D1732905

Me and Sugar Boy

Enjoy!
Melanie Bell

MELANIE BELL

Copyright © 2021 Melanie Bell
All rights reserved
First Edition

Fulton Books, Inc.
Meadville, PA

Published by Fulton Books 2021

Credits:
Colten Bell: Designing the Cover
Author, Melanie Bell: All of the Illustrations

ISBN 978-1-63860-012-1 (paperback)
ISBN 978-1-63860-013-8 (digital)

Printed in the United States of America

"I want to give thanks to God for giving me the vision and courage to write. My husband Dart, who encouraged me and always supported and believed in my efforts. I bounced a lot of ideas off of him, Colten and my 2 daughters, Mariah Narup and Dalton Bell.

I want to give credit to my son Colten, for being such a wiz on the computer. He converted my water color for the cover illustration and made it usable.

Special thanks to my good friends;

Jo Weaver, who read everything I sent to her and gave me her honest opinions, which I took to heart.

Beth Woodliff, my best friend and confidant, who has a heart of gold and a great sense of humor, always offering a positive outlook.

My good friend Liane Johnson, who played the "devil's advocate", whenever I needed grounding or encouragement.

Last but not least, my friend Harmony Downman, for introducing me to the Welsh pony and offering me Rudy, aka Sugar Boy. Rudy will forever be my inspiration and best friend and I will forever owe Harmony for this delightful and exceptional pony, who taught me to live!

I would like to thank Chelsey Bates for walking me through the publishing process and Fulton Books for believing in my story and taking the chance on an unknown writer.

I will forever be indebted to my parents, Maddry Myers Godfrey and Janice Rose Johnson Godfrey, for all their love and support. They showed me endless love and patience, as only great parents can do with a headstrong daughter. They inspired me to believe!"

Rudy, aka Sugar Boy

My first impression of the world was that it was cold and wet. Overstimulation would only begin to describe the mixed emotions I felt in those first few moments of life after birth. Everything was new and confusing.

As I was peering at my surroundings, I realized I was experiencing sensations I had never encountered—sight, sound, smell, and physical awareness. None of these new senses were very comprehensible. I was in a total state of confusion. I guess it was Mother Nature that finally kicked in to clarify my predicament. I felt an urgent desire to move.

Nearby, my mother softly nickered to me, reassuring that all was fine. She slowly stood and turned to where I was lying, briskly licking me to warm my chilled body. I felt she was a bit too rough at times. I desired to lay still and try to warm myself in the fluffy straw bedding. I later discovered that her invigorating licks helped me wake up to the newness of life. I needed to move.

My natural curiosity eventually overcame the confusion of birth. I began to experiment and coordinate my long legs, kicking in multiple directions at the same time. I learned that balance was a concept that I had never encountered. Even so, I felt the urgent compulsion to move.

Ever so slowly, I attempted to organize my legs and make my first effort to stand. This did not turn out as I expected. I found myself collapsing into a jumble heap. It was a total disaster! I felt defeated and even more confused. Why could I not achieve what Mother Nature was requiring of me?

My mother nicked reassuringly, so I tried repeatedly, often tumbling into the stall walls. Hm, seems these barriers are trying to impede my progress. I glanced at Mom with questioning eyes.

She responded with a savvy look that encouraged me to continue with my battle.

Her constant nickering was so comforting with each failed attempt. She instilled in me that "standing on my own four feet" was very important.

I continued with the conflict. Although watching me struggle must have appeared quite comical, she never once offered the slightest suggestion of a chuckle.

Failure after failure eventually wore me out. I needed to rest for a moment. This idea of standing was more complicated than I first realized. Nothing on my body wanted to work together. It was like God had thrown together a miscellaneous bunch of items and expected them to unify and cooperate. Glancing at Mom, I saw she was also resting. Okay, it must be all right to pause and regroup.

I have discovered that I am not very patient. Even so, God has also blessed me with a clever mind. As I rested, I assessed all the new experiences and tried to devise a new plan.

After a short reprieve, I was prepared to try again. This time I was successful. Wobbly, but successful. I was standing! What a great sensation! Mom opened her eyes and smiled warmly at my success. So this is life.

Chapter 1

The look of the eagle.

—*Gallant Fox* by C. W. Anderson

I guess everyone has dreams and aspirations that drive them to keep living and striving to reach long-awaited goals. I don't know if they ever reach them or even believe it is possible to have those dreams come true. Life tends to get in the way. What starts as a child's innocent belief in obtaining the impossible becomes a life of reality, filled with jobs, family, and the endless search for security.

This is the story of my personal quest to follow my childhood dreams and how a special pony made it possible for me to believe in myself, my dreams, and God's prescience in my life. Rudy assisted me in my belief that there is more to life than the obvious.

There is a possibility of reaching dreams through hard work and planning, that God uses whatever is necessary to help you live the life He has planned for you; that God wants you to succeed and experience His love firsthand.

As a child, I found a deep love for animals, especially horses. Living in the city, I never really had any contact with horses but nevertheless developed a true and abiding love for these beautiful creatures. These animals were grace, beauty, humor, and love all wrapped into a magnificent creation.

It was my older sister, Ginger, who had a profound effect in developing my equine interests. Being the oldest, Ginger was a mentor who both inspired and terrified me. She was a strong individual—smart, confident, and a definite leader. She was also an avid reader and soon had me following in her footsteps, reading every horse book I could find.

Early on, my favorite books were *Billy and Blaze* books, written and illustrated by C. W. Anderson. I would look at these books for hours, admiring the wonderful pencil renderings of Blaze and Billy. I longed to be capable of drawing as well as C. W. Anderson and creating such wonderful stories. I read them over and over, wishing I could be the child in his book and find a pony like Blaze, so devoted and beautiful.

I have been told that everyone can draw at an early age. Those who succeed are the ones who continue to draw and pursue the development of that talent. C. W. Anderson inspired me to continue to sketch and create my own stories of horse and pony farms. Hours were spent in preparing elaborate layouts of farms and creating fantasy ponies. I did not know then that these hours spent in creative drawings and future farms were to set the direction of my life.

Later C. W. Anderson would once again inspire me in another book, the true life story of *Gallant Fox*. This tale of a 1930s racehorse is where I first heard the phrase, "the look of the eagle."

Not really knowing what that was, I filed it away in my mind to be pulled out and used again some forty years later. It now seems like a lifetime away, but the "look of the eagle" became apparent in its meaning on a spring day in May 2007 when I first met Rudy.

I was in a transitional period in my life with horses. I was disillusioned with the breed I had been involved with for over thirty years. Being a "traditionalist," I had a tendency to favor keeping the original breed specs and felt this particular registry was getting too far from the intended ideal. The "grassroots" farms were being pushed out, and unfortunately, I fell into that category. Disenchantment had me looking at other options.

Ponies had always been my favorite equine. Growing up, I was fortunate to be acquainted with Mr. B. B. Stroupe, a unique individual and an accomplished horseman. An elderly gentleman, he was a mentor with wise information on life and equine endeavors. He loved the Hackney ponies and soon recruited my sisters and me to ride his high-strung, powerful show ponies. If nothing else, these ponies and Mr. Stroupe taught us to ride.

We also absorbed many of Mr. Stroupe's personality traits: "Never settle for second best and never give up!"

Since I was looking for another equine possibility, maybe a pony breed was my best option.

It was during this time period that I received the "Select Pony Sale" brochure in the mail. It never occurred to me how or why this was mailed to me until much later.

I eagerly looked at all the ponies featured in this quality sale. I was mesmerized by the beauty of these ponies as well as the outstanding prices. This led me to investigate the breeding on these ponies. To my surprise, I found that all but two of the over thirty ponies listed were either Welsh or half Welsh.

I often say, "I don't believe in coincidences." The timing of receiving this magazine during my search for another direction for the farm convinced me that this was no coincident.

I was instantly infatuated with the beauty and versatility of the Welsh breed. I decided to find a local breeder with a suitable stallion for breeding to my existing mares. I could not afford a pure Welsh, but at least I could start developing some half Welsh ponies.

After a Google search, I located a Welsh breeder, Blueridge Welsh in Fletcher, North Carolina, just two hours away. I quickly made an appointment to visit the farm. With my daughter Dalton in tow, we made the drive to Fletcher. There in the Blue Ridge Mountains we discovered a wonderful farm and acquired a new friend in Harmony Dowman.

On our initial visit, Harmony warmly greeted us. She took us on a tour of her facilities and showed us her many fabulous ponies. I was overwhelmed by their beauty. They look just like my childhood "fairy-tale" ponies. I was instantly in heaven and knew for the first time in my life that this was the breed of pony where I belonged.

On our tour, we eventually ended up at her mare and foal pasture, where we were delighted to see three beautiful mares with their adorable foals. It was here I first saw and understood the old horseman's saying, "The look of the eagle."

He was a large colt, only three weeks old, but with the arrogance and swagger of a much older horse. It was his eye that caught and held my attention. He had the steady gaze that even to this day says, "I have everything under control." I was surprised and delighted to see such a confident young colt. He immediately exhibited his curious and confident nature and walked right up to the fence.

Rudy, aka Sugar Boy

More visitors! This usually means treats! I think I will just "ease" on ahead of everyone and check out Harmony and the other two. I have never seen them before, but then Harmony is always bringing in new folks to see us. First one to the visitors wins the most treats!

Mel

As Harmony introduced the mares and foals, I could not keep my eye off that large chestnut colt. He was so bold and appeared to be friendly. I had never felt this attraction to any other horse in my entire life. I was mesmerized!

Rudy, aka Sugar Boy

What is it about this lady? She keeps staring at me. Mom says it is not polite to stare, yet I kind of like the look in her eye. She seems to appreciate something about me.

Mel

As Harmony educated us on their personalities and pedigree, I ask if they were friendly and if we could pet them. She readily agreed and said the large chestnut colt was the friendliest. His name was Blueridge Rising Star, aka Rudy. I could tell he was quite certain that he was named appropriately. One look told me that he felt he was entitled to all the attention and praise and was truly a rising star.

I have trained and been acquainted with hundreds of ponies and horses in my lifetime. Many are quite memorable...some for notorious deeds, some for delightful personalities, and some for great achievements. I can appreciate all horses for their individuality, beauty, and strength in body and spirit.

The humblest, most unattractive horse still offers the human soul a gift of appreciation and source of awe. Shakespeare so appropriately gives voice to this, "When I bestride him, I soar. I am a hawk: he trots the air; the earth sings when he touches it; the basest horn of his hoof is more musical than the pipes of Hermes." Even Shakespeare could not describe the feeling I felt when I first saw Rudy. This colt entered into my soul as a kindred spirit. We were meant to be.

I walked up to him, and to my surprise, he stood his ground. He never showed the slightest attempt to leave. As I reached to rub him, he seemed curious to search me out as well, rubbing his nose over my hands and arms. If there is love at first sight, then this was it.

Rudy, aka Sugar Boy

No treats in sight. This must be a rubbing and scratching session. I kind of like this lady. She seems to respect my space and does not "overdo" the affection thing. Maybe she is one of those "horsemen" that my mom told me about. They seem to understand our ways of communicating.

Mom also told me that you don't encounter too many of them now a days. Must be because horses have become a luxury item… whatever that is. When we were a "necessity," it was a different story. At least that is what Mom told me. She also said that for the most part, we have a much easier life than back in the olden days.

Mel

As we exited the pasture, I asked Harmony about the colt, knowing good and well I could not afford him. She quickly told me he was already sold and had been purchased in utero. I was relieved and disappointed. How could I justify trying to buy an expensive colt? We were struggling to raise three children and transform a run-down cow farm into a suitable stable.

Even so, Rudy stayed on my mind as we exited the pasture. I would be returning to Blueridge Welsh with my future broodmares in June.

Breeding time came around, and once again, Dalton and I headed back to Blueridge with two of our best mares, Dovie and Brandy. Both were maiden mares and were ready for their first foals after achieving very successful show careers. They also exhibited the temperament to safely pack young children over a hunt course. We felt this was an important trait to establish in our breeding program.

Anticipation, insecurity, uncertainty, and excitement at the possibilities were all commingling in my brain. Dalton and I were ecstatic at our decision to venture into the Welsh pony world. We chatted all the way up to the farm, sharing our opinions on the stallions and the possible future foals.

Once we arrived and settled the mares into their paddocks, I asked to see the perspective sires once again. Rosmel Notorious, her senior sire, greeted us with the welcoming attitude and confidence I sought in a stallion. He pranced and danced around his paddock, exhibiting the presence of a fine show pony.

Moving on to the barn, we approached the stall of Rosmel Scarlet Legacy, her young three-year-old stallion. He was my first choice for breeding: stunning, correct, and a gifted athlete. Everything about him said, "Look at me! I am the gold standard of quality."

Glancing down, I noticed a small plastic bat outside his stall door. As Harmony opened the door, he charged at the opening with bared teeth and pinned ears. Whoa, not the way I expected him to behave. Harmony picked up the small bat and chased him to the back of the stall.

I observed his nervous and agitated behavior and instantly begin questioning his personality. Legacy was aggravated, but did not appear to be mean. How much of this was learned behavior, and how much was his personality?

I am a big fan of John Lyons, the internationally famous horse trainer from Colorado. His method of teaching has changed my entire approach to horses and my training methods.

I firmly believe in his novel concept of training from the horse's point of view. Training with him has helped me to work with many problem horses, perceived to be mean but actually mishandled or misunderstood.

John clarified many questions that had me stumbling around for years in my attempt to uncover the best techniques for the horse and rider. I knew I could help Harmony with this difficult, young stallion.

Cautiously I asked Harmony if I could work with Legacy for a moment. She quickly agreed, and I picked up the plastic bat. Just like before, Legacy charged at me as I entered his domain. This is typical behavior of a young stallion who has no idea of his place in the "pecking order" of the world.

As soon as he was within reach, I quickly popped him across the nose, more for sound effect than pain. This startled him, and his ears came forward as he retreated to the back of the stall, glancing around as if to say, "Whoa, no one has ever done that to me."

That was all it took to get his attention and all I needed to pursue a relationship that was in the proper sequence.

This is not a "boss and employee" concept as much as it is a "respect between partners" idea. I have found that often horse owners get the wrong perspective in their relationship with their horse, causing numerous problems in horse behavior. I often quote the comment spoken in the "Horse Whisper" by Robert Redford: "I don't help people with horse problems, I help horses with people problems."

As Harmony informed me about some other handling problems, I continued to work with him on these stumbling blocks. We soon settled into a cooperating relationship where he understood what was expected, and I was able to recognize when he was ready for the next step. Communication!

Legacy's cooperation dictated when I could proceed. My job was to break everything down into small steps, making it easier for him to figure out the correct response.

Gradually, Harmony saw all that was possible when approached from Legacy's point of view. In my opinion, the horse's point of view is the only thing that matters in the training process; that and my self-control and communication skills.

It was this small demonstration of my training skills that led me to the deal of a lifetime and a true friendship with Harmony and Legacy.

John Lyons also helped me in my relationships with people. As with the horse, I learn to approach people from their point of view.

I understand what is important in a relationship, whether with people or horses. Both were born with certain personality traits and have a value system that they have learned to live by. You have to accept them as you find them before you can try to establish a change in their behavior. After all, you cannot change the past and can only deal with the present situation. Especially with horses, if you look into their past, you find yourself making excuses for their behavior rather than addressing the current problem. It limits you on helping the horse find the solution.

As we prepared to go home, Harmony asked me if I was still interested in Rudy. She informed me that the original owner had been involved in an accident and had broken both of her arms. She was unable to handle a weanling and had requested to have her money back and nullify the deal. I could not believe what I was hearing. I was scared and excited, as this was my dream colt. Now we had to discuss money, definitely not my strong suit.

Seems God had a plan in place, and Harmony and I were able to reach an agreement. She was so impressed with my work with Legacy and needed him started under saddle. I readily agreed to train and show her young stallion for six months. In return, she would sign over the colt, and I would own Rudy, my first pure Welsh…my dream colt.

Chapter 2

Be all that you can be, not who you are.

—John Denver, "The Eagle and the Hawk"

I think we all reach that time in our lives when we realize our own mortality. Usually this is after the enthusiasm of youth and the routine of middle life have evaporated. Whatever dreams we had, have either been forgotten or changed to the point of frivolous fantasies to help us escape reality.

Society as whole seems to encourage this attitude of indifference and lack of imagination. "Play it safe" has transformed the American way of life to apathy rather than adventure.

Before my encounter with Rudy, I was living that same mere existence. Making ends meet was my primary motivation in life. I had few dreams, and the ones I embraced had been pushed aside. I hoped for a miracle to let me pursue them again sometime in the future.

Life was too busy. I was falling behind in my attempt to keep up with all the new developments in technology. I struggled with its effect on the job market. I had no desire to compete in the technology job field. Even so, I recognized it was going to take over every aspect of our lives. My art talent was becoming archaic in the workplace. Anyone could become an artist with the help of a computer program.

I still had my horse training as a backup, and I continued to work with Legacy. I knew that this was going to be my salvation from the ever-changing work place. Legacy gave me the hope and satisfaction of seeing a job well done.

Harmony was pleasantly surprised to see how his behavior had improved. He was such a pleasure to show, and his successes had me receiving acknowledgment for my talent. I found him humorous and playful, making me yearn to have Rudy home.

I was approaching fifty years old when I first brought Rudy home from a fall show in Gainesville, Georgia. Harmony and I had arranged to meet there and exchange Rudy for Legacy. I would be showing both ponies at this Welsh pony show.

Up until this time, I had kept Rudy a secret from my husband. Dart was clueless about the arrangement between Harmony and me. Sometimes it is necessary to keep quiet until the timing is right. Dart may say that there is no such time, but I knew he had been a little bit deceptive when we were first married. He needed an expensive piece of equipment for his wood working business. We were literally living "hand to mouth" in a rented trailer. Although we both worked, we had no money to spare. Even so, he had a "once-in-a-lifetime deal" on this machine and purchased it without consulting me.

One day, while I was visiting him in this workshop, I passed right by this machine several times. Dart was on pins and needles and hoped I would not notice this new hulking piece of equipment. After all, he shared this shop space with another wood working friend. Somehow, he kept me distracted for weeks.

On one of my visits, just out of curiosity, I asked him about the function of this particular apparatus. He could stand it no longer and came clean with me about the purchase. He even laughed when he told me I had passed by it for months. When I confronted him about leaving me in the dark on this purchase, he replied that I was so stingy on small supplies he knew I would have a tantrum over this big financial acquisition. He also included the fact that he was paying for it with his woodworking jobs, taking nothing out from out household budget. He was right. I had been very tight with our money. I could see where he would be hesitant to tell me about this purchase. Besides that, we both were newlyweds and had never had to ask permission for anything.

Thinking back, I felt this past purchased of his would even the scales with my current "purchase."

God knew what he was doing when he brought Dart and I together. We are both strongly independent, creative people with a lot of talent and a short supply of business acumen. Together we make a respectable living and support each other's eccentric activities. Dart has always recognized my tendency to be impulsive. Often this has led to several bad decisions on my part. Even so, he has been very tolerant of my spontaneous behavior. The trust between us is occasionally strained, but basically, we accept the other's judgment. Knowing his tolerance level, I knew this may be pushing his limit a bit.

My friend, Cynthia, and my daughter Dalton encouraged me to proceed with bringing Rudy home without telling Dart.

"You have so many chestnut ponies, he will never notice," they explained. "Even if he does notice the extra pony, it will buy you some time to come up with an explanation.

You know the old saying, "It is better to ask for forgiveness than permission."

Taking heed to Cynthia's and Dalton's advice, I was encouraged to take the risk and proceed home without forewarning Dart. Even so, I knew he would be upset when he found out about Rudy.

Rudy arrived at the showground in Georgia, just a few hours before his first class. He cautiously walked off the trailer and Harmony handed his lead to me. Longing for him to relax, I led him toward some grass, hoping he would graze. I knew if he ate grass, he would relax and start to accept his new surroundings.

Rudy, aka Sugar Boy

What the... I have never been this scared in my whole life. Mom had given me the "heads up" weeks ago about what was about to transpire in my life. She overheard Harmony talking about my future with a new owner. I just did not think it would happen this quickly. I am only a "weanling." That is one step up from being a newborn. What is Harmony thinking?

In fact, Harmony just weaned me last week. She took away my "pacifier," so to speak. If ever I was hungry or stressed, I could always depend on Mom to feed me and make me feel secure. Now what am I supposed to do?

I just knew I would be on Harmony's farm until I was at least a year old. Ponies are supposed to be a little more secure as yearlings.

I know that I am on the "headstrong side." But right now, I am not ready for leaving the only home I have known.

I already miss my Mom desperately and want to be back home with her and the other ponies. Will I ever see her again? Will I ever see all my friends and my former wonderful home?

I have encountered many new things this past week. Most I accepted. I watched Harmony lead my mom using devices called halters to control our destinations.

At first, I was not too fond of this, as I have always chosen my own way. Even so, I was smart enough to know when to pick my battles, and this one was a minor one. I quickly decided that halters were acceptable.

Mom seemed to be good with it, so I tried to follow her example. Did not mind them so much, but the horse trailer…that was another story.

Mom walked on first. I questioned her, but she kept encouraging me. I nervously jumped on after her. I sure wasn't going to be left behind. It wasn't too bad, a bit close quartered, but Mom reassured me that it was safe.

Then we were asked to back off. This made me question just what was Harmony up to? I was relieved, however, to find out that the trailer was not a permanent situation.

Later that day, Mom told me that trailer rides would take me on new adventures. I retorted that I really did not need any "new adventures" in my life and I was quite happy at home.

She smiled and said life is always full of new adventures. She encouraged me to try everything at least once. She wanted me to live life to the fullest and assured me that I was going to grow up to be something special.

Reliving that conversation, I now recognize that I am experiencing one of those "new adventures," thanks to an inexhaustible trailer ride. I try desperately to grasp on to her words of encouragement. I am actually feeling fear for the first time in my life. I so desire her presence and the wisdom she imparted to me.

Even though I am fearful, I am still a bit curious. Curious or not, the long ride was disturbing to me. It made me feel like I have no control over anything. I do not like feeling out of control.

From the beginning, when I learned to stand on my own, I have always felt sure of myself. Confidence was so easy and always had me one step ahead of the other foals. Now my self-assurance has vanished.

I struggle to remember Mom's advice. I can almost hear her explaining the relationship between the horse and the human. She told how it could be very complicated and required trust and understanding on everyone's part.

"Son, always do your best. Try to figure out what your new owner expects of you. If you ever have a question, just stay calm," she explained.

"What is a new owner?" I asked.

When she saw the question in my eyes, she responded, "Rudy, they are the people, like Harmony, who will take care of you after you are separated from me. They will be responsible for all your needs. Hopefully you will be blessed with a good one."

"Good owners will love you like I do," she continued. "They make sure you have everything you need. I pray you will find the right owner and have a wonderful life. You cannot stay with me, so prepare for the day when you will be on your own. Remember... I will always love you and your siblings."

I am in tears, thinking back to that conversation. I recognize I am obliged to put on a brave face. I must make my mother proud and do my best to remain calm.

My only traveling companion has been an older gelding, who seemed to take everything in stride. At least he was friendly, and I tried desperately to mimic his confidence. He was very experienced in adventures and trailer rides and kept me entertained with his many stories. I appreciated his calming influence.

Pulling into the showgrounds, I neighed softly to see if anyone would give me an answer back. I could smell the other horses but did not recognize any familiar aromas. When we come to a stop, I anxiously awaited the unloading process to see what would transpire.

Remembering Mom's words of wisdom, I was determined to face this new adventure with confidence.

As Harmony backed me off the trailer, I saw a beautiful facility with white fences, white barns, and several riding rings…much larger than those at home. There were people everywhere and many ponies in various stages of preparation for the show.

So this is my first big adventure! I am going to be a show pony!

Oh wait. There is that woman and her daughter who came to visit Harmony way back in the spring. Why is Harmony handing the lead to her? She seems nice enough, but I don't know…

Using Mom's advice about staying calm, I tried to do my best, allowing this woman to take my lead.

I assumed this was my new owner. Following her to a grassy lawn, she offered me a free rein to graze. How did she know that this was just what I needed? I haven't had any grass since I left home! I took that as a good sign.

Mel

When I first took Rudy's lead, I felt like I was walking on clouds. He seemed to be so composed compared to the previous foals I had handled. Even Dalton, who can be quite the skeptic, was surprised at his quiet demeanor. I knew that time would tell if this was a false sense of security or a true expression of his personality.

I asked Harmony how Rudy handled the trailer ride, and she said they took their time and had no incidents on the way down.

I was relieved to see he was relaxed and did not seem stressful. After all, he had just been taken from his mom, trailered from the mountains of North Carolina to Georgia, and dropped off at a busy showground. I appreciated his great outlook. I also felt it was a confirmation of the confidence I had seen in the three-week-old colt with the "look of the eagle" back in the spring.

We still faced preparation for this evening's halter class. Being his first time off the farm, all this commotion could overwhelm him and bring out undesirable behavior. This could result in injuries to him, me, or anyone around whenever we attempted to clip, wash, and possibly braid his mane. Time would tell.

Clipping and washing came with a just a few incidents, Rudy pulling back, trying to escape, and falling onto my friend Cynthia's lap. He lost his balance in the wet, soapy wash pit and fell right on top of her, collapsing into soggy heap. I earnestly inquired about her safety as they both struggled to untwine. Laughing hysterically, she assured me she was okay.

Even with all the excitement and atmosphere of urgency, Rudy continued to exhibited the same confidence I had noticed the first time I saw him. It was obvious to me that he was smart and learned easily from his errors in judgment. I was amazed to see this maturity in such a young pony. After all the preparation, it finally came time for his debut into the show ring. Rudy's class was to be held in a covered arena under the lights.

Since it was September, we would be making our way to the arena in the shadowy darkness. Emerging into a well-lit venue from this murkiness could startle most beginner show horses, much less a young colt. Rudy calmly accepted the situation and followed me willingly to the brightly lit arena.

There we encountered a ring full of young weanlings and yearlings, some behaving and some, well, let's just say they were not enthusiastic about showing.

Being six inches taller than the rest, Rudy was definitely the standout because of his size. He calmly gazed at the other foals with a pensive interest, but showed no sign of fear or insecurity.

When the class was called to order, most of the youngsters trotted in with minimal handling problems. I panicked. Remembering that Rudy was barely halter broke, I wondered if he had been taught to trot on the lead. Too late to worry about that now. Hoping for the best, we made our way through the entrance gate.

Trotting was not going to happen, even when the judge tried to encourage him.

Rudy, aka Sugar Boy

Look at all these ponies! Wow, this is so cool. This place is amazing! People, ponies and so much excitement. I can hardly contain myself. Maybe I will just give a little "kick up" to impress the others.

Mel

I did the best I could in the situation but was totally caught off guard when Rudy decided it was time to play. Even so, I was glad to see he had a little spunk.

Rudy, aka Sugar Boy

Must have been the wrong move. My handler reprimanded me for that one…but what did she expect? Everyone else is having a good time! I am really confused as to what I am supposed to do in this situation.

"Do your best," my mom's words reverberated in my mind.

Mel

The class seemed to go on forever. As I waited for the placings, I prayed Rudy would stay under control. I knew so little about this young pony. He seemed to be calm and alert, but with young foals, that can change in a heartbeat.

Glancing at the other foals, I felt like we had a good chance at placing well, even with our "minimal" trotting and our kicking outburst.

As the placings were revealed, Rudy received a disappointing fourth in his halter debut. Even so, I was excited to show my own Welsh pony. I could envision the champion he was destined to be. Maybe the next show would provide a better placing. At this time in his life, the halter classes are so important. He really needed to place well if he intended to be a breeding stallion.

As we head back to the barn, my thoughts now turned to Dart and the trip home. Cynthia, Dalton, and I had discussed our plan for sneaking him home and into the barn. It would be late and dark, hopefully so late he would be asleep. If we succeeded, it would be a few days before he discovered another chestnut pony in a field full of brown horses.

I kept telling myself, "Better to ask for forgiveness than permission."

We arrived home late at night. Cynthia succeeded in sneaking Rudy into the barn without Dart being alerted to the new arrival. I was temporarily relieved. I was so exhausted from the weekend of showing and only desired my own bed and a good night's sleep. The Rudy issue could wait until morning.

The following day, Rudy settled into the pasture. He easily made friends in in the mixed band of mares and geldings. I was grateful for his confident and friendly personality, so no conflicts ensued to draw Dart's attention.

Dart eventually discovered Rudy, and boy, did I have some explaining to do. After presenting my best arguments, including the machinery incident early in our marriage, he just shook his head and walked back to his workshop. Time heals all wounds, as does forgiveness.

From the first time I saw Rudy, I knew he would establish our breeding program. With this in mind, I choose to raise him in a natural herd situation. After seeing how easily he was accepted into the herd, I knew he had the right personality for our breeding stallion.

Social skills learned in the herd would better prepare him for his future, both in the show ring and the breeding barn.

Rudy, aka Sugar Boy

My new home was better than I had expected. Plenty of new friends and room to roam. I have never had so many playmates. We boys have some great times galloping and playing on the rolling hills and frolicking in the woods. I enjoy our vigorous playing and look forward to the expulsion of all my youthful energy. It is exhilarating and makes me feel strong and unstoppable!

The young fillies will occasionally join us, and some of them are quite athletic…but I have learned to avoid the mares. We call them "the old ladies" because they are so grumpy whenever we try to include them in our frolicking. None of them are as kind as my mom. The other youngsters encourage me to ignore them.

After all our running, we eventually move out into the sun and lay down in the warm grass. As I lay waiting on sleep to come, I think about my new owner, Melanie, and her daughter Dalton. Both seem to be one of those "horsemen" my mom mentioned during our daily talks.

I am reminded of this conversation about their uncanny ability to communicate on our level. It is like they can talk and listen to us, recognizing our questions and answering them. The fact that they recognize we have a question is remarkable. I am so grateful that these two seem to understand me.

They work with me almost every day, even if it is just visiting in the pasture. The treats have disappeared, and I do miss those. I have discovered I really like the affection almost as much.

It seems respect is very important here, and I feel respected! Maybe not from the old ladies, but I respect them!

Slowly I feel the sleep creep into my mind and body. My dreams reflect on the past and race toward my future. Life is good.

Mel

Our first two years with Rudy were uneventful. He joined into the herd as if he had been born there. I was comfortable leaving him in the pasture until the late winter of his coming two-year-old year. So far, the mares had shown no interest in him as a stallion. He, too, seemed to respect them and showed only minor interest during the cold months.

On an early cold March morning, I was horrified to discover him breeding a senior citizen mare who was infertile yet obviously still sexually active. Banner was eighteen years old and had never been able to conceive.

I was not worried about a possible foal. In fact, I figured she would teach him proper breeding manners quicker than I could, so I quickly dismissed the incident. Nevertheless, I recognized it was time to take him out of the herd before he achieved his first foal. Show season would soon be starting up, and he needed to concentrate his efforts elsewhere.

Little did I know that in the following spring, Banner would give us a beautiful colt from this union. His son, D. F. Sneak Preview, aka Rueben, would become a champion Dressage pony. Nor did I know that Rudy had also impregnated our black Arabian mare, Sallee. She would actually give us his *first* foal, D. F. Dulché. Rudy definitely had his own agenda in the fall of the previous year. How did I miss that?

Moving into spring, we started preparing to show in the WPCSA breed shows. Now a two-year-old stallion with breeding experience, thanks to Banner and Sallee, I was concerned about a possible personality change. He would be showing in halter classes judged on his conformation, presence, and manners.

To our surprise, Rudy was so calm and stoic in his classes it often masked his real beauty. His complacent attitude in halter classes often had judges calling him a "slug." These placings reflected his poor showing, and I begin to question my decision to leave him a stallion.

His entrance trot was a disaster. This was the judge's first impression, and Rudy resembled a "plow horse," never showing any excitement or elegance. He would stand calmly, but refused to square his legs up. I knew he was capable. It was almost like he was trying to show just how ugly he could make his presentation. As a handler, I felt inept and amateurish.

Rudy, aka Sugar Boy

Another halter class. I despise these classes. Look at all those doltish ponies out there blowing and showing off. I am not a fan of this type of behavior. After all, I am more than just a pretty face. I only act that way when I am playing with my buddies. Mel has made it quite clear that I am not allowed to rear, bite, kick, or strike in public.

I don't understand Mel's reasoning behind participating in these halter classes. Everything I attempt to deter her just makes her more determined to continue with this nonsense. I have been to enough shows to know what really constitutes a pony's worth—performance classes! Performance actually takes intelligence and athletic ability. Under saddle classes—that is where I will shine. I can hardly wait to get started.

Mel

I often listen to music to inspire and encourage me. John Denver is one of my favorite recording artists. His song "The Eagle and the Hawk" caught my attention one day when I was trying to convince myself that leaving Rudy a stallion was the right thing to do. The line "be all that you can be and not who you are" led me to believe that Rudy would one day show his true colors. Presently, we were in the "what you are" stage of his life.

It is often in this phase of pursuing your dreams that you make rash decisions based on other people's opinions. Judges' halter placings did not support my vote of confidence in Rudy. I don't remember how many times I was told to geld him and sell him as a hunter pony. He would bring big bucks, and our financial worries would be over.

It might have been a smart business decision, but that mode of thinking had no place in my dream of Rudy's potential to be a great Welsh stallion. I still believed Rudy would make a difference in the Welsh breed.

To this day, I thank God for not bowing down to the pressure of "what others thought." I chose to listen politely and then made my own decisions. I decided to follow my dream and see where Rudy took us.

Dreamers, artists, writers, musicians, and dancers—all live by different standards. We are motivated by things unrevealed to the more practical individuals. Most of America choose the safe way with good careers and financial security, but the dreamers often "follow the path less taken." We are not always successful, feeling like failures when compared with society's standards of success. Nevertheless, we still dare to dream, to pursue and believe in things unseen. It would be two more years before I saw in Rudy the promise "of all he could be."

Chapter 3

Be so good, they can't ignore you.

—Steve Martin

Rudy was now a three-year-old stallion. His physical changes were astounding. Even Harmony commented on how much he had matured and improved.

God decided to change his color as well. No longer a red chestnut with flaxen mane and tail, Rudy now had a rich liver-chestnut coat with silver working into his previously yellow mane and tail—the proverbial horse of a different color.

I was looking forward to starting him under saddle and seeing where it was going to take us. I felt this was going to be a pivotal year for us.

Previously I had sent Rudy off to a trainer in Leicester, North Carolina.

Still keeping with the notion of retaining Rudy as my breeding stallion, I recognized he needed a job to help maintain his raging hormones. He was only two, so driving was the only option I would consider for this young stallion.

After weeks of groundwork, it came time to hitch him up for the first time. The young trainer recruited a good friend, an older horseman from Asheville to help her with this initial hitching. This gentleman mostly worked with Belgium drafts. He actually was employed at the Biltmore House, driving the tourist around the estate. This kind gentleman gave me Rudy's first compliment.

He said, "Rudy has to have some Belgium in him somewhere because this pony has way too much sense!"

I still consider this one of Rudy's biggest compliments and my first real vote of confidence in my decision to keep him a stallion.

Fortunately, training has always been one of my assets. There are breeders, and there are trainers, but there are few who are able to encompass the whole package. With the help of my daughter Dalton as an assistant, we began the under-saddle process with Rudy in the spring when he turned three.

I use the round pen reasoning process created by John Lyons. John has always been a big influence on me since I had the opportunity to ride in three of his clinics. After a humbling experience in the first clinic, I found out I could not learn enough from this dedicated horseman and amazing teacher. Through his mentoring, I discovered the horse to be an intelligent and reliable partner when trained from the horse's point of view.

John's process enabled me to proceed at a very quick rate, depending on the horse. Much of the ground-level work had already been established in our handling of Rudy from his early childhood where I discovered he was quite clever. Raising Rudy to trust and respect people had established a crucial foundation.

Rudy, aka Sugar Boy

Mel is taking me to the round pen. The other colts told me this day would come. I have seen this many times before with the older ponies. I am finally getting to pursue what I know I was born to do—performance classes! I have seen so many at the shows and just know that I can perform better than anyone.

I am also eager to show Mel that I am as good as she perceives. Been hearing some of her discussions with other people about me. I know they are wrong, but she is still unclear on my future. I can tell she is a bit worried about her assessment of me.

With all her knowledge, I can't understand why she would doubt herself. For the first time in my life with her, I recognize that

I will have to take the lead in showing her just how much we can accomplish.

Mel

As I turn Rudy loose in the round pen, I pray that all will go well. I also seek the patience and wisdom to really communicate with him from his viewpoint.

Rudy, aka Sugar Boy

As we start the training process, I seem to be proceeding correctly. I wish the other ponies would quit running and trying to distract me. I know they are doing it on purpose because they want me to mess up.

I have to stay focused or Mel will scold me. I am not a follower, but when everyone is having such a good time in the pasture, it is hard to ignore them... I must pay attention. I really want to do what is right.

I am so glad she is patient and actually encouraging me to run. Whoa, now I have to turn and go the other way. That was easy enough. Whoa! I have to turn again. What the heck? How did she do that? I am actually starting to concentrate.

This constant changing of direction reminds me of life. Never know where it is going to lead you. Funny time for me to get philosophical.

Okay, I am getting a bit tired of this constant changing of directions and running. See if I can slow down to a trot.

Trotting is better, as I am getting a bit winded. I look to her for directions. Can I stop now? She recognizes that I am asking the correct question and lets me stop to catch my breath.

I look as she approaches me. What is she wanting now? Calmly she rubs my head, turns her back to me, and walks away.

Are you kidding me? She did all that just to rub my forehead?

Here she comes again, same thing, only this time she kind of hangs with me, rubbing my sweating body and talking in sweet tones, telling me what a good boy I am.

I am content to just stand and rest. My lungs have finally convinced my brain to pay attention and figure out what she wants.

Mel starts introducing new items to me: blankets, lariats, and finally the saddle. I stand quietly, as she does this. I have no desire to repeat the running marathon.

Nothing has hurt me thus far, and I really don't want to return to the rail. Standing appears to be a good option.

Thinking back, Mel has never really hurt me in the past, except maybe once when I bit her. She bit me back on the nose. Boy, was that a surprise. Never felt that urge to bite her again.

Oops, she is back. Better pay attention.

I am officially saddled. Not sure how all this came about, but I am okay with it. What? Now she wants me to go back on the rail and work some more?

Jeez Louise. Maybe I do feel a little bit of rebellion now that I have my breath back. Let me see if I can unload this saddle.

Mel

I watch closely at everything Rudy does during his training process. It is important to assess what is serious and what is normal. The small bucks with the saddle are normal. I actually like to see that happen at this stage. I want him to understand that the saddle does not come off and it does not hurt him.

Rudy, aka Sugar Boy

Okay, I get the message. This is a semi permeant fixture. I am not going to waste any more time with bucking. Let's just get on with the program.

Mel

Before I mounted Rudy for the first time, I remember what John said about the first mount. He told me to "step back and make sure you have done everything possible to ensure the horse is quiet and relaxed," indicating he has no fear. I was also reminded that I needed to mount and get off so the horse knows that it is only a temporary situation, and he does not have to wonder if I am a permeant attachment.

The first time I mounted Rudy in the round pen was such an exciting and unforgettable moment. I was finally on the beautiful young colt I fell in love with three years ago. At that time, little did I know that we were about to embark on the ride of a lifetime and the fulfillment of a dream.

The next few months were filled with days of repetition and trail-riding. I was constantly asking Rudy for more. He learned to give to bit pressure, turn, and stop from my seat adjustments and give to pressure from my legs.

Soon we were side-passing, backing, and opening gates. The more I asked, the more he gave. He always appeared to be looking for a new challenge. He inspired me to ask more and seldom questioned the new challenges. I was excited to see this side of his personality and looked forward to the show season.

Show season finally came around, and Dalton and I felt like we had fulfilled all the possible training scenarios. Rudy's gaits were becoming more balanced, and I eagerly anticipated going to our first show. I felt confident in his abilities and his manners.

Our debut show that year was in Raleigh, North Carolina, at a small Welsh breed show. Surprisingly, Dalton volunteered to be the "test pilot" on Rudy in the open English pleasure division.

Rudy astonished us both by winning two of the three classes, making him the English pleasure champion the first time out! I was thrilled. Secretly, I had my doubts and believed it was beginner's luck.

Rudy, aka Sugar Boy

Wow, it felt so good to finally give Mel and Dalton the recognition they deserve. They have faithfully believed in me from the beginning. I knew it all along, just had to wait until I could work under saddle to prove to them that they were correct in their assessment of me. Now all the others better take notice!

If I can just get Mel to grow along with me. With all her knowledge, why does she lack confidence in herself and me?

Mel

That year we continued to show, and we continued to win. Rudy was always champion or reserve champion, regardless of the judge or location. I had never experienced this kind of success. Even so, my insecurities and doubts kept creeping into my mind. It was like I was almost afraid to be so successful. I had dreamed but never experience this level of achievement, and I kept anticipating the downfall.

Occasionally we had setbacks—flat tires regularly on the trailer, money problems, and constant bickering between Dalton and myself—but as a whole, we enjoyed the show season.

Rudy remained composed and helped me handle many discouraging challenges. I was amazed at what I was absorbing from this young stallion, who seemed to accepted whatever life had to offer. He seldom questioned situations and continue to bring joy to Dalton and me.

The following year, Rudy turned four, and we were ready to start him over fences. The Welsh pony is known for their jumping abilities, so it was only natural to pursue that venue with Rudy.

We engaged a trainer to help us train him correctly. Karim was a former Olympic level rider from Morocco. He had worked with my eldest daughter, Mariah, when she was showing our half Arabian mare, Dovie. I loved his teaching methods and was looking forward to introducing him to Rudy.

We hauled him over to ECC, Equestrian Center of Charlotte, for our first lesson. At four he was a stunning stallion, fit, glossy, and quite the athlete. I just knew Karim would love him. After all, he saw quality horses and ponies at all the big shows.

Rudy, aka Sugar Boy

Okay, this is new. Definitely not a show, but looks like a pretty nice facility. I am always up for a new adventure with Mel and Dalton. Looks like Dalton will be riding as she is already dressed. Not show attire, so that is a bit different.

Mel

While Dalton and Rudy made their way to the ring for a warm-up, I walked over to Karim to inquire if he had any questions. He asked what we had in mind for this pony. I told him hunter over fences at the Welsh breed shows. He could not show as a stallion in the USEF pony classes.

He nodded his head then said, "He is not the hunter type."

My first response was, "Are you kidding me? Can you not see the quality in this pony?"

Was I really hearing that Rudy was not as good as I previously thought? After all, this trainer had seen international competition and he should know. I was dumfounded.

As I stewed, he proceeded with the lesson which included the majority of flat work and a few rounds of some trot poles and cross rails. I hoped I was not "barn blind" because I kept hearing that same statement over and over, "He is not a hunter type." To me that registered as a major fault in Rudy. After all, Welsh are recognized as the ultimate hunter pony.

Watching Rudy and Dalton work, all I could see was a fantastic pony doing some amazing flat work and taking every new challenge with confidence and eagerness. Rudy never refused or spooked at any of the obstacles in the ring. Even when other riders came in, Rudy stayed on task. Surely that accounted for something.

Although I was disappointed at Karim's opinion of Rudy, I decided to continue the lessons as I knew Dalton would benefit from them and Rudy would enjoy the change of venue.

Over the course of several weeks, Dalton and Rudy showed great improvement in gaits and jumping. He was a natural jumper, and Karim begin to see the magic that I saw in Rudy. He came up to me after one of the secessions and gave me the second most important compliment on Rudy that I have ever received.

Karim said, "I don't know if it is him or her, but these two are the best I have coached in this area." Quite the compliment for the pair as he trained in a well known equine community.

I quickly forgave him for his "he is not a hunter type" comment. Rudy had won over another important and trusted trainer. I now had two votes of confidence in favor of my decision to keep him a stallion.

We continued to show, and eventually we were ready to experiment in the over fence classes. Our first jumping class would be at a Welsh show in Southern Pines, North Carolina.

The judge was John Almond, a well-known breeder and highly favored judge from Maryland. This would be the first encounter between John and Rudy, but not the last. At this time, I did not know how important this judge would become in promoting Rudy's career. It was also at this show that Dalton and I would see a new developing aspect to Rudy's personality. Up until this time, Rudy had always been very focused and agreeable. Suddenly Rudy became a stallion.

Right before the low hunter classes, Rudy became agitated and nervous in the warm-up. There were several young ponies acting up. The tension in the practice area was so thick you could cut it with a knife. I saw Dalton struggling with control and Rudy intentionally ignoring her requests.

I called her over, and she was nearly in tears, frustrated and angry.

Dalton was a very accomplished rider, even as a young teen. Rudy was showing a side to his personality that actually scared and confused her. She begged me to scratch him from his jumping classes.

I told her, "Give me the pony."

She quickly agreed and begged me not to make a scene. Clearly, she knew the side of me that can lose control.

Rudy, aka Sugar Boy

I am so nervous. This is a new feeling for me, and I do not like it. Why do I feel like I have so much energy? I have no confidence in myself or Dalton.

I feel like I have to confront the other ponies. Are they really challenging me, or is it my own insecurity? When did I acquire this self-doubt? I can now relate to what Mel feels at times.

Here comes Mel, and she is not happy. I can see the rage. Conflicting thoughts are confusing me. Fight, flight... Why can I not focus?

Mel

I quickly took hold of Rudy and led him away from the chaotic warm up arena to a private spot where we could "have a conversation." I knew I had to control the situation and myself. Believe me, I am not known for my self-control.

Luckily, I remember John Lyon's words of wisdom. He always stressed that whenever you have a problem with your horse, you need to return to a place in your training where the horse can be successful. You can then work back up to where the problem started and reteach him on a positive note.

Since correct leading had been emphasized Rudy's whole life, I knew he could be successful in that area. I started with the basics and soon had him working successfully in his leading exercises.

Once he started to respond, I mounted up and continued with the principals he had learned in his early training: give to the bit, step through the shoulder, back, drop his head on command, and walk off on a loose rein.

Rudy and I eventually reached a conclusion, and we both agreed on how the classes were going to proceed. He calmed down, and I called Dalton over to us.

Rudy, aka Sugar Boy

I feel so much better. The familiarity of the training exercises really brought me back to my old self. I don't like whatever happened back there in the warm-up and despise that feeling of loss of self control. That is not me.

Thinking back, I remember Harmony talking about Legacy and his hormones. Not sure what that was about, but I think I am now experiencing the effects of hormones. They must be very powerful because they caused problems in Legacy, and he was a very strong willed, confident individual.

Either way, I am ready to compete. I will show everyone just how good I am over fences!

Mel

I finally talked Dalton into competing in the classes. Rudy had a good go and even won the reserve championship in his debut over fences.

John Almond became a Rudy fan at that particular show in Southern Pines. He recognized that Rudy was "too good to be ignored."

Chapter 4

*If you do not go after what you want, you'll never
have it. If you do not ask, the answer is always no.
If you do not step forward, you'll always be in the
same place.*

—Unknown

Taking the first step out of your comfort zone is probably the number one reason for abandoning your dreams. We all get caught up in the comfort of routine and desire for security in our lifestyle. After all, security poses little risks and offers a small possibility of failure. Security requires few or no changes and offers more of the same safe circumstances every day.

The fear of failure and of the unknown kept me struggling for years with personal insecurities and lack of confidence. God gifted me with a wonderful family, great childhood, and an abundance of talent. So why was I fearful to pursue many of the opportunities He provided in my life? Why do any of us doubt ourselves?

Rudy was brought into my life for a reason. What I have gained from this relationship with Rudy is the confidence to take that step out of my normal routine. To observe an animal handle so many different situations with confidence and the desire for adventure inspired me to change my attitude and try his approach to life.

I still find myself amazed at how most animals live day to day without fretting. It is almost like they know more about life than we do. Sure, they become stressed in certain circumstances, but as a whole, to them life is good. They do not look back or forward but live in the moment.

Recently a beloved equine veterinarian, "Dr. Bob" Gochnauer, passed away. It was a shock to the whole community. In his service and on his memorial, they quoted from the Bible, the book of Job:

> But now ask the beasts, and they will teach you; and the birds of the air, and they will tell you; or speak to the earth, and it will teach you; and the fish of the sea will explain to you. Who among these does not know that the hand of the Lord has done this, In whose hand is the life of every living thing, and the breath of all mankind? (Job 12: 7–10)

When I first read these verses, I was searching for answers. Looking closely at my relationship with Rudy, the meaning became apparent. God uses whatever it requires to guide you; to expose you to the life He intended for you. He wants you to succeed, live fearlessly, and be part of His plan.

Rudy taught me to accept myself and be satisfied. I learned it was okay to be successful, and it was okay to fail. He challenged me to be all I could be. He inspired me to live fearlessly.

It was now 2012, and I was desiring to do great things for the Welsh Pony Breed. I was so enamored with the ponies and Welsh exhibitors. They knew how to be competitive and have a good time while doing it. I had never encountered competitors who wanted to assist you at shows.

In retrospect, I decided to see what I could do to entice people outside the breed, to experience the Welsh pony. I aspired to show that the ponies were much more than children's riding ponies and the breeders were openly friendly and willing to accept you.

I thought my best way to expose the Welsh pony to outsiders was to write an article about the Welsh pony and find a magazine to publish it. Talk about getting out of your confront zone; I am an artist, not a writer. Even so, I could not resist the urge to write this article.

With the help of my oldest daughter, Mariah, and her husband, Danny, we pulled together a pretty decent article called, "Welsh, Not Just for Kids." It was published in the *Carolina Hoofbeats* and was my debut into the world of writing.

In preparation for this article, I talked with several important breeders and many Welsh enthusiasts from all over the USA. Janice Early was one of the breeders who gave me great insight into the breed as well as introducing me to her amazing stallion, Flying Diamond the Bailef.

Bailef is a Section B Welsh stallion that competed successfully in the Extreme Cowboy Races, an American Quarter Horse and Mustang Makeover sponsored event. This small 13.1 hand Welsh pony and his adult rider competed almost entirely against horses.

Bailef achieved a national top ten in both the United States and Canadian National version of this extreme test of a horse and rider's abilities over enormously demanding trail obstacles.

He also placed third out 1,500 contestants in the televised show, *America's Favorite Trail Horse*. Needless to say, I was impressed with this mighty, mini contestant.

I was able to meet Janice in person at the 2012 AGM, the WPCSA annual convention. This forum is held every year in a different location. In 2012 it was held in Raleigh, North Carolina. Dalton and I agreed that we needed to be there. Our goal was to meet some new Welsh breeders from different parts of the country. Since Rudy had only been shown in our district, we wanted to expose him to new exhibitors.

At this time, we were only recognized by a few local breeders. I prayed that some of the locals would attend. This was a big step for me, out of my "security box." I had to face my fear of the unknown.

Before going, I noticed on line that the registry was having a stallion auction to raise money. Breeders were donating stud fees to be auctioned off on Saturday night at the close of the session. Going out on a limb, I sent in Rudy's stud fee donation. Because we were so new and inexperienced in the Welsh breed I knew no one would recognize Rudy's name. We probably would not even receive a bid. I consoled myself with the idea that it was the thought that counted.

Arriving at the convention, it was just as had I feared, full of strangers. Even so, we bravely attended many of the different events that were offered. It was at one of these seminars I met Janice Early. She was giving an impressive PowerPoint presentation on Bailef and all his achievements.

We quietly entered and found two vacant seats next to a woman who was already seated. As we settled in, the woman quickly introduced herself as Margret Almond, John's wife. I could not believe this coincidence. She recognized us because John had been quite impressed with Rudy at the show he judged in Southern Pines. How random that we would sit right next to her.

After the presentation, I quickly moved to the line to talk with Janice. She was super nice, and I was "starstruck" at getting to meet her in person. Bailef, in my opinion, was legendary. This encounter was a changing point in my breeding program. Instead of focusing on the hunter pony aspect, I decided to pursue a more versatile pony, one that could do it all and do it superbly.

Deb Branson, our Carolina Club president showed up later in the day, and I felt relieved seeing a local breeder. We soon found out she and several other locals would be conducting the driving clinic. Dalton and I learned quite a bit that day at the driving clinic and the open forum, the two other events we decided to attend.

We chose to sit out the evening dinner as we both were over whelmed by the daytime activities. I was also "chicken" to see if anyone would buy Rudy's stud fee donation. Once again, fear stopped me.

The following morning Dalton and I made our way to the elevator, anticipating a good breakfast before we started back home. I was surprised to see John Almond also waiting at the elevator. He said hello, which thrilled me as I did not even think he knew we existed. He proceeded to tell me that he had bought Rudy's breeding the previous evening. I quietly thanked him. I could hardly hold in all the exhilarating feelings that were trying to explode inside me. I could not believe what I heard!

As John left us to join his party for breakfast, we hurried off in the other direction, amazed at this turn of events. Rudy was going to have a breeding in Maryland the following year! His first foal outside of North Carolina!

Over breakfast, Dalton and I discussed the convention and all the things we learned. Were we ever surprised when Dr. Ruth, the WPCSA president, came over and took time to speak to us personally. She actually knew our names! She was friendly and encouraging. Maybe we were in the right breed. Our former breed association had never offered this type of hospitality and for sure no encouragement.

After breakfast, we hurried to our room to prepare for checkout. I just had to call Harmony and tell her about John's bid on Rudy's stud fee.

Harmony was overjoyed at hearing the news. She told me, "He must really think highly of Rudy. John does not breed to just any stallion. It was quite an honor for him to buy his breeding."

I knew then that Rudy must be special. This notable judge was taking a chance on an unknown young stallion after seeing him at only one show. I was thrilled to learn that he acknowledged Rudy to be an exceptional pony.

After the AGM, I was even more enamored with the Welsh pony, their owners and exhibitors. I decided that Dalton and I needed to go as far as we could go with Rudy in the Welsh breed shows. For the first time since I had joined the Welsh breed association, I started entertaining the idea of going to the Welsh National Show in Tulsa, Oklahoma. That became my goal.

Hard work and perseverance were requirements when one sets a lofty goal. I knew that the goal I had set was not going to be an easy one to achieve. I had no idea where to start. The realization of the cost almost over whelmed me. Doubt led to stress, which led me to almost abandoning this dream.

Yet Rudy was a constant reminder to keep me focused. How could I deny him the chance to be the best? After all his successes, how could I refuse to give him this opportunity?

Every morning, when I started out to the barn to feed, Rudy eagerly neighed a good morning, often trotting up to his gate to greet me as well. It was almost like he knew what was in the works. He was ready to take on the challenge.

During this time, I started calling him Sugar Boy because he was always so friendly. Coincidently, I learned from my ninety-year-old aunt Audrey that my dad was nicknamed Sugar Boy as a child. Seems as a young boy, Dad liked to get into the sugar bowl. I was starting to notice those darn coincidences.

Rudy always wanted to be a part of whatever was going on at the farm. Often I would let him out into our enclosed yard to eat grass while I fed the other ponies. This led to some interesting insights into his personality.

Our yard contained not only the house but two large shops as well, one on either side of the house. The closest to the house was Dart's woodshop, where he made cabinets, furniture, and electric guitars. The other consisted of my art shop, a pool table, and various items stored for different reasons.

It was during these grazing periods that we discovered Rudy's curiosity about everything. Dart would be working in the shop, and Rudy would climb the two concrete steps and enter through the door. Seems he just wanted to check things out.

To Dart's amazement, he did not spook or show any fear, even with the machinery running. After looking around, he would exit the way he came in and proceed to resume his grazing. This happened frequently, and Dart would tell me at the supper table, "Rudy came to visit me again today."

Rudy also looked in on me at my art shop. I was painting a mural on some canvas spread out on the floor when I heard his hooves on the concrete. I looked up to find him watching me paint, taking care not to step on the canvas. I asked him what he doing, and he casually turned away and went back out the door.

Sugar Boy was quick to figure out where the ceiling fans were on the covered stone deck. I found him standing there one hot afternoon, enjoying the breeze. I was amazed to see he had climbed the three stone steps to make himself at home with the five dogs that were napping on the deck.

Rudy also figured out where our bedroom window was located. One morning Dart and I were watching TV in bed and eating breakfast. Rudy calmly walked up to the window to check out what we were doing. Dart joked and said we must have Mr. Ed reincarnated.

With his natural curiosity and confidence, it became clear that Rudy could do more than the traditional pleasure classes. I began to entertain the thought of training him for the trail classes. Trail classes eventually became a regular part of my training with Rudy. It piqued his interest and ended up helping me at the shows.

Whenever his attention would wander at a show, I would find some trees to jog around, poles to step over, or areas with ditches to navigate. He would soon start to focus, and we would have a successful class.

Trail obstacles helped him loose his "need" to create excitement at the shows. Too bad we did not discover this before "the show from hell."

Chapter 5

Problems are not stop signs, they are guidelines.

—Robert Scheuller

The show from "hell" was going to be our debut to the Northern States region, where they had larger shows. We were ready to travel farther to compete against different ponies and expose Rudy to new exhibitors. Our first northern show was in Front Royal, Virginia, about six hours away.

Dalton and I were to leave on Friday and take Rudy and his firstborn son, Dulché. He would have a good traveling companion in Rudy, and since it was his first show, I hoped Rudy would assist him in adjusting to the trailer and show experiences.

On Thursday morning, Dalton woke up with a fever, headache, and sore throat. She was extremely sick, and I knew we had to see a doctor. Making the appointment, I questioned if we would be able to make the trip.

She was diagnosed with strep throat. The doctor said a shot of penicillin would clear it up in twenty-four to forty-eight hours, and she should be feeling better. Just great. Not even on the road, and we were already having a problem. Was this an omen?

I asked her the next morning if she felt like she could make the trip. She agreed to go along even though I saw she felt horrible. I let her sleep the majority of the way up and hated that she missed our first trip through the Shenandoah Valley. The scenery was spectacular, and the weather was perfect. She missed all the fabulous farms and homes that doted the amazing landscape.

Arriving at the showground round two, we were delighted to see such a charming show facility. I learned it was formerly an old remount station for the calvary, now renovated to a lovely show venue surrounded by mountains. I was starting to get excited about this new adventure.

We parked the trailer and began the process of finding our stalls and unloading our menagerie of show items, feed, and ponies. Show management had been considerate of our stallion and gave Rudy a corner stall which gave him some privacy on one side.

We quickly turned to preparing the ponies for the show, beginning with the baths. Washing was a small problem, as the facility only had hoses and no wash pit or way to tie the ponies while washing.

Dalton had a choice between holding the ponies or washing. She readily chose to hold the ponies partially to avoid getting wet. She was still sick and possibly had a low-grade fever. I agreed she was better suited to hold ponies as well.

We decided to bath ponies together to save time and keep our washing spot. I proceeded to soap up Rudy and Dulché. Luckily during this process, they had grass to eat. It helped Dalton keep the ponies distracted while I scrubbed and hosed off the soap.

We received quite a few stares during this process, as it was not the normal procedure to wash a stallion with another horse in such close proximity, not to mention both being held by a young girl. Knowing Rudy, I had no doubt he would behave. I had always treated him like any other horse.

I also learned this from John Lyons. He said, "Treat a stallion like any other horse, just remember he is a stallion."

Making special efforts to isolate stallions only creates a false narrative. Stallions, like all horses, are social creatures. They need contact, and I had been true to that bit of knowledge. Raising Rudy in such a manner taught him how to conduct himself in most situations.

Once we had the ponies clipped, washed, and prepared for the show, we cleaned stalls while they ate their grain then headed to the hotel. We looked forward to showing the next day.

Aware that Dulché would be showing first in the half Welsh halter, we were grateful that we did not have to be at the showgrounds early in the morning.

The show started at eight, and Dulché's class was at the end of the morning session. Halter classes take a long time, and usually the half Welsh halter classes start just before the lunch break. We opted to take advantage of this and sleep late, which actually meant seven in the morning.

The following morning, we arrived at the showgrounds according to our preconceived scheduled time. As we pulled in next to our trailer, I was surprised to see Deb Branson, our club president, hysterically running toward me.

I had no idea that she was coming to this show. After that surprise, she gave me another one that was just the preview to our show from hell.

"Mel, your class is next!" she cried.

"What?" I replied with a questioning look.

"They have a severe storm warning this afternoon, so they decided to start the show at seven. No one knew where you were staying, and we had no way of contacting you," she answered. "What can I do to help?"

"Oh crap. Dalton, get dressed and I will get Dulché ready," I screamed. "Hurry! Deb, please help Dalton if she needs anything and let the show officials know we are coming!"

Dalton was still moving a bit slow. She felt weak. Being a teen, morning sleep was important to her. A groggy Dalton kicked it into high gear and jumped into the trailer dressing room to change into her show clothes.

Down at the barn, I literally knocked the shavings off, put on Dulché's show halter, and ran him to the ring, where the officials were waiting for us. Dalton grabbed the lead and trotted him in as if nothing was wrong. I was so proud of her.

Dulché placed a disappointing fourth against some meticulously braided ponies turned out to perfection. I could not help but look at Dulché's lackluster turnout and feel like we had failed him by being late.

Rudy and Dalton were to exhibit next in the English pleasure junior to ride. At least we had time to prepare. Taking Dulché back to the stalls, I looked at the class sheet to see when Rudy would go in his first class. He was to show after a short break. We took our time grooming him and tacking him up. Dalton looked eager to mount up for a warm up secession. Since they both were ready, I agreed to let her go a little early.

I felt good as I boosted Dalton onto Rudy's back. He seemed eager, and she appeared to be ready to school him and see how he behaved. He schooled beautifully in the warm-up. Several young riders spoke to her and told her that he was going to win. I was pretty confident as Dalton entered the show ring full of ponies and young riders.

As she came around, I could see she was still pretty pale, but determined. The trot looked good, although I noticed that Rudy was hyped up. Dalton was struggling, but so far, she made him look good. They looked professional and like the champions they were.

The judge called for the canter. What happened next was a totally unexpected nightmare. Never in my wildest dreams would I imagine this would occur.

Rudy looked like bucking horse of the year as Dalton asked him for the canter. It was so unexpected and violent I gasped out loud. I prayed Dalton would hang on until she could get him back under control. I worried that he would unseat her and bolt loose among all the young riders. What a disaster.

The judge quickly called for a halt, and all the ponies eventually transitioned down and stood still. Dalton was able to bring him down to the walk and rode to the center of the ring to ask to be excused. The judge readily agreed.

Dalton kept her composure til she exited the gate. Then she broke down and cried, screaming that she would never show this pony again. I grabbed Rudy's reins at the gate, with Dalton in tears. I was so angry at Rudy. How could he choose this show to embarrass us and endanger my daughter? We had wanted to impress the new exhibitors with his wonderful work ethic and quiet nature. Boy, that sure fell flat.

Dalton slid to the ground and begged me not to make a scene. Hm, that sounded familiar. I held my temper and decided on a plan on the way back to the trailer, one that would reprimand him without embarrassing me or Dalton.

Arriving at the trailer, I changed the tack to my western show saddle. I borrowed Dalton's helmet, mounted up, and headed to the other warm-up ring. Rudy was going to work off some steam...mine and his.

On the way, I noticed an open gate to a field that was on the side of a small, grassy mountain next to the ring. I ditched the warm up ring and rode into the hilly pasture. If he had all this energy, I was going to help him work it out.

Rudy, aka Sugar Boy

Oh no. I don't think I have ever seen Mel this mad. I really did it this time. I just don't know what came over me. I just wanted to impress the ladies, and boy, were there some nice ladies in there. Those stupid hormones again.

Is she really going to ride me up this huge, steep mountain?

Mel

I turned Rudy's nose toward the top and yelled, "Hiya!"

Rudy responded, and we galloped full speed up the steep hill. Reaching the top, I could hear Rudy's heavy breathing. I was not swayed by this show of exertion.

I turned him and trotted him back down the hill, all the time calling him asshole and other well-deserved names in my mind for his embarrassing outburst.

One more time I told myself, "Hiya," and off we went!

The next thing I knew, I was flying through the air, thinking to myself, *Did this fool just buck me off?*

When I hit the ground, I landed with the saddle, lying on my back with my feet facing uphill. As I sat up, I was surprised to find Rudy looking straight at me.

Rudy, aka Sugar Boy

Yep, She's okay. I am getting the heck out of here and giving her some time to cool off.

Mel

I almost cried as he turned and ran back up the hill and over the top and out of sight. I could hear the announcer saying, "Loose pony on the grounds!"

My humiliation was complete.

Dalton and a local couple came running up to see if I was okay. They had seen the whole thing. It turned out, my cinch strap had broken, and the whole saddle came off during our second wild charge up the hill. I was relieved to know that he had not bucked me off.

Desponded, I started up the hill to see if I could find Rudy. I did not know if it was a hundred-acre field or a twenty-acre field, and I only hoped it was the latter. All I knew for sure was that he was over the top and out of my sight. Not a good thing when you own a stallion.

Arriving at the peak, I saw Rudy grazing beneath a tree next to a wooden fence. He raised his head to look at me. Under my breath, I threatened to kill him if he ran off. I also prayed he would let me catch him and not run back down the hill or off into the wild blue yonder on this side of the hill.

He stood his ground and carefully watched my approach, pretending that the grass he was eating was just too good to leave.

Rudy, aka Sugar Boy

Well, I hope she has had enough time to cool off. I know I messed up, and I am fully aware of her temper. She has learned to laugh at most of my infractions, but this one, umm...maybe not.

It was not totally my fault. I know I should not have exhibited my bucking skills in the ring, but I had nothing to do with the saddle breaking. At least I stayed and made sure she was not hurt.

Knowing her as well as I do, I also know she needs a cool-off period. Me getting out of her sight for a while seemed like a good idea at the time.

I am going to take my chances that she is ready to start over… again. Wonder if she will notice I stopped at this wooden fence in case she wants to ride back.

Mel

Rudy let me catch him, and luckily, the bridle and reins were not damaged. How convenient he stopped where there was a fence to help me mount. I was sure not going to walk all that way back.

Coming over the hilltop, I saw Dalton and the couple gathering up my saddle and saddle pad. Upon reaching them, I assured them that we were okay. I slid to the ground so that Rudy could carry the tack. I also thanked them for their concern and joked about the incident.

Arriving back at the stalls, I glanced at the sky and saw some really ugly clouds building up rather quickly. The wind was also picking up at a rapid rate. So this was the storm they were worried about. I was so grateful we were not still on the hillside, looking for Rudy.

The storm blew in with a frightening strength that had me stressed, so I knew the whinnying ponies were filled with fear. The rain was so heavy you could not see ten feet in front of the barns. It completely obscured the beautiful mountains from sight. Although it was midafternoon, it appeared to be almost dusk.

Glancing at Rudy, I saw him calmly eating his hay. Dulché was nervous but soon adapted Rudy's attitude and munched down on his hay as well. I was relieved to see this, as many of the ponies were still extremely upset with all the lightning, thunder, and heavy rain. The noise was incredibly loud.

Dalton and I looked at each other. We had never experienced such a strong storm over an extended period of time. When would it end?

During this time, I needed a distraction. I decided to search for a cinch to replace the broken one on my Western saddle. I turned the tack trunk upside down, hunting for this very important part of the saddle. No cinch, no show. Filled with despair, I reached the conclusion that we did not have a spare.

With the barn filled with the noise of the raging storm, I decided to seek help from the other exhibitors. I proceeded down through the barns, asking strangers if they had an extra cinch. I knew this was going to be a long shot. Most Welsh ponies only show in English attire, so the odds were against me.

As luck would have it, I met a Western rider who happened to have a spare. She offered to get it after the storm cleared because it was in her trailer. I promised to return it after the Western classes. Graciously I thanked her and hurried back to our stalls.

Finally, the storm moved on, and the sun soon cleared out the vicious squall. We heard the first call for the show, starting with the Western pleasure division. I retrieved my borrowed cinch from the fellow exhibitor and raced back to our stalls.

Wouldn't you know it. This was my debut in the Western pleasure division, and the rings were a sloppy mess. Not my idea of ideal conditions for our debut. Another omen?

We had about twenty minutes to tack up, get dressed, and warm up. Dalton worked on Rudy as I quickly made the decisions not to wear my chaps or cowboy hat. After his last episode with the bucking horse stunt, I opted for a helmet and jeans.

Originally, I decided to try Western at this show since Rudy was still under five years old, enabling me to transition him to Western riding using the same style bit as his English bridle. I could also use two hands on the reins.

After five, the Western ponies were required to neck rein and use only one hand on the reins. We had not accomplished that skill yet.

Dalton called for the bridle, and I turned to the totally upside-down tack trunk on the tack room floor. Rolling my eyes, I started to search through the mess I had created. Eventually, I located the Western bridle with a full cheek snaffle bit. Those who are not familiar with this bit may not appreciate the humor in this next disaster.

A full cheek snaffle bit has a broken center in the mouthpiece with large vertical pieces on the outside of the round rings where the reins and headstall are attached. As I pulled it out of the tack trunk heap, I could not believe what I was seeing. The bit was so tangled up in the reins and metal parts it looked like one of those metal puzzles from the dime stores that you spend forever trying to untangle.

Never in my forty-plus years of riding have I had such a catastrophe with a bridle. Dalton was urging me to hurry up as they were calling for the class to start. I was so angry I was about to just quit and miss the classes. Consequently, I remembered we *had travelled six hours* to get here, and I was not going to leave here with a bad impression of Rudy's behavior.

Dalton came to my rescue and worked through the puzzle as I stressed about traveling to the ring in all the mud.

Bringing Rudy out of his stall, completely saddled and bridled, she urged me to just mount up and go.

Once mounted, I headed to the ring, trying to figure out where Rudy was "in his mindset." I did not want a repeat performance of Dalton's class. I was too old to ride a bucking horse in the mud. At least it might be a soft landing should he make an attempt.

As I warmed Rudy up, I was relieved to see he seemed amiable as he worked in the slippery conditions. Only two other ponies in the Western division, and that would help me keep my distance if he should decide to act out again. I prayed he would behave, as I did not want to fall in this swamp of a ring.

Finally, I heard the call to open the end gate for exhibitors to enter. Entering the ring, Rudy seemed to be pretty stable and only occasionally lost his attention to the other ponies. They were both seasoned Western ponies, but they were also mares. He and I both knew what that meant. It was my job to keep him focused and his job to respond to me.

I thought back to John Lyons asking me a question at one of the riding clinics. "What was my cue to get my horse's attention back while under saddle?" At that time, I quickly realized I did not have one. I had never even thought of that before. John suggested to teach my horse a cue to regain his attention. It consisted of teaching the horse to give to the pressure of the bit by releasing him every time he responded correctly. This is so important for many reasons, refocusing a horse being only one of those. That was my cue, and I used it every time Rudy's mind began to wander to the lovely mares.

Rudy, aka Sugar Boy

Okay. This is the new deal, Western pleasure. I actually like this style of riding as I don't have to put forth the same energy. Much more laid-back.

Boy, is this ring messy. Not too fond of mud, but this may add to the adventure of this new class.

I feel like a real horse from the old days, working a ranch. Mel has worked with me, and I have heard her brag about my "cow horse" sensibility to her friends. Not sure what a ranch and cow horse really are, but I understand the horses are very talented in the things they have to do. Seriously hard work.

We have trail ridden and been through some pretty tough brushes and creeks, along with riding up and down steep hills. I actually like the "trail-blazing" that all the other riders complain about when they ride with Mel. They constantly give her a hard time about making new paths and pushing the limit.

Oops. She just signaled me to pay attention. Here comes one of those beautiful ladies. I need to try and focus after the calamity this afternoon. Somehow, I have to redeem myself.

Mel

The class went better than I expected, and Rudy placed second after a "quick start" in the first lope. Only two more classes in this slop. Maybe we will survive and I will come out clean. Rudy will have to be hosed off, if he looks anything like the other ponies.

Surprisingly, Rudy had two really good showings in the remaining classes. He worked through all the mud and water like a trooper. I guess all the trail-riding and trail-blazing paid off. I was so excited to win the last two classes, and also our first Western pleasure championship!

The judge approached us as we were leaving the arena after the last class. She suggested I show him in dressage. She loved his fluid gaits and round frame. I thanked her and entertained the thought of another venue to pursue. She was the first of several judges who would later give me the same advice.

We were finally through for the day. Arriving back at the stalls, exhausted, disgusted, filthy, wet, and miserable. Yep, 'bout sums up the day. At least we had redeemed ourselves in that last division. Now we needed to finish up our chores here and head for the hotel. All we could think about was a cleanup and good meal.

We fed the horses, settled them into the stalls, and started for the hotel with good intentions of relaxing after a hot shower and good food.

Arriving at the hotel, we had no idea that the calamities of today would continue to plague us. Entering the front door, we did not feel the cool blast of air from the air-conditioning. We also noticed it was dark in the foyer. We stopped by the attendant at the front desk and asked what was wrong. She informed us that the power was off and had been since three that afternoon.

Dalton looked at her phone and saw that it was now six. Three hours without power? When would it be restored? Another omen?

The attendant told us the same storm had damaged several blocks of the city. It was anyone's guess when they would get the power restored. Just Great! Dalton and I just looked at each other in disbelief. Using her cell-phone light, we made our way down the darkened interior hallway in our wet, muddy clothes. We were miserable.

Since we could not take a shower, we had to settled for a towel off and clean clothes. We decided to wait for a short period of time. After thirty minutes, we elected to head out to find somewhere to eat. Surely there was food venues that were not affected by the outage.

Luckily, we found a restaurant with power. Over a warm meal, we talked about our crazy day and all the bad luck. This conversation led us to the decision to cancel our Sunday classes. Dalton was exhausted, I was humiliated and tired, and the ponies needed to get on the road home as soon as possible. We could use the excuse of her school on Monday morning and a six-hour drive to make our early exit seem plausible.

When we arrived back at the hotel, we were so pleased to find the power back. Now we both could have a good night's sleep—stress free due to the cancellation of our classes in the Sunday show, happiness over our new Western pleasure championship, and some redemption of our stallion's reputation.

The showground was bustling with activity when we arrived to start feeding and packing up the trailer. I pulled out our small red wheelbarrow to help carry the larger items back to the trailer, while Dalton fed the ponies. It was not the sturdiest wheelbarrow, but it was a gift from a friend and sufficient to do the job.

As we were packing the smaller items, I came back to our stalls to find a strange man working on my wheelbarrow. I was a bit confused. Maybe he was mistaken and thought it belonged to someone he knew.

He glanced up as I approached, unsure how to handle this situation. He quickly saw my uncertainty and responded.

"I could see you needed a little help with this wheelbarrow. I have my toolbox here for just this reason…in case someone needs a repair. My wife is busy braiding ponies, and I'm trying to stay out of her way. I am not any help in that department. Hope you don't mind. It gives me something to do."

I have been accused of "never knowing a stranger." I took the opportunity to visit and make a new friend. I was astonished at his hospitality. In this respect, the "northern exposure" show was a pleasant surprise after enduring the embarrassment of the Saturday show.

Dalton and I appreciated the friendliness and found that once again, Welsh pony people are willing to help, even if you are a competitor.

Finally packed up, we loaded the ponies and pulled out of the showgrounds, anticipating our trip home. We planned a lunch break and hoped to be in Iron Station, North Carolina, before the evening feeding. Dalton and I thought we had left all the bad issues behind in Front Royal, Virginia.

We laughed about all the craziness and looked forward to seeing our farm and sharing the unfortunate tale with Dart. I was sure he would get a big laugh out of it.

We stopped for lunch at Burger King just as church was letting out. This slowed us down as the lunch crowd was bigger than we had anticipated. Even so, we filled up with food and fuel and hit the road again.

When we reached I-77, I felt like we were home. Only forty-five more minutes! Wrong! I heard a loud pop and felt the trailer swerve. I knew in an instant that we had just blown a trailer tire. Being in the center lane on a busy interstate, I sweated as I carefully maneuvered the trailer over to find an exit ramp.

In retrospect, you have to know that I have a history of trailer flat tires. My previous trailer enabled me to become quite adept at changing tires. Now my new trailer was insisting I continue my education on changing tires.

Front Royal was our first trip with our brand-new, though slightly used, three horse slant-load gooseneck trailer…my dream trailer. I could just hear Rudy saying, "Here we go again."

Rudy, aka Sugar Boy

You have got to be kidding me. New trailer, and a blow out on it! Hate to tell you, Dulché, but we're are in for a long stop. Hopefully, they will feed us our supper when Mel finds a place to pull off and change the tire.

Mel

We limped on down the highway until we found an exit. Luckily this one had a gas station with a cover area where we could park in the shade. At this point, I just looked up to God and said, "Really?"

Parking under the shelter, I quickly ran into the station office to ask for permission to stay there until we could change the tire. It was hot, and we did not know how long it would take. The attendant readily agreed.

Although thoroughly a "pro" at changing tires, I soon found out that life had slipped me another one. The beautiful chrome rims also had beautiful chrome lug nut covers. Puzzled, Dalton and I looked at them and wondered, how in the world do we get those off? No matter what we tried, we could not budge them.

Dalton called Dart and explained the situation. Since we were in the area where his brother Robin lived, he told us that he would call Robin to help us and to just wait on him. Do not tear anything up!

While waiting for Robin, Dalton went into the dressing room and found the tire-changing kit as well as the trailer manual. Voila! When in doubt, read the manual!

Sure enough, it explained everything, step by step, on how to change the tire. We were able to remove the lug nut cover, the chrome rim, and start working on removing the lug nuts. Couldn't budge them. They were on so tight. It was definitely going to take a much stronger person than me and Dalton.

God sent his angels in good time, and a Good Samaritan arrived to help us loosen the lugs. He was a truck driver, of all things, so he was just what we needed.

He helped us remove the tire and replace it with the spare. Just as he started to put on the lugs, Robin arrived and relieved him of that duty. I felt so relieved to see a familiar face. We thanked them both and soon were back on the road headed home.

Unbelievable, was all I could think. Thank God the rest of the trip was uneventful.

Chapter 6

There are two ways to live: you can live as if nothing is a miracle; you can live as if everything is a miracle.

—Albert Einstein

I am a true believer that the world has a plan. I cannot accept that all the things we experience and observe are just random acts. I believe there is a higher power and a purpose to all things seen and unseen. I am constantly reminded of this whenever I am fortunate enough to see a foal born, hold a baby, or see an act of kindness or a show of compassion.

The year is now 2014, and it started off with an event that would affect me the rest of my life. My beloved mother, Janice Rose Godfrey, died on January 3 after a bitter twelve-year battle with Alzheimer's. Although it was a blessed relief to her suffering, it was a heartbreaking affair for our whole family, especially my dad.

My mother and father were the true love story that everyone hopes to experience. They met at a tender age when she was fourteen and he was sixteen. She told her mother the day they shared their first kiss that she had met the man she was going to marry. True to her word, she did just that. They shared sixty-one years of a wonderful marriage.

That first kiss started with Dad's friend Lester Rudisell sitting with his girlfriend, Janice, watching a high school basketball game. Dad came out of the locker room after showering from a post season football practice for a bowl game.

Spotting them, he decided to join them since he had a secret crush on her. After the game, they went to have a soda at the drugstore then escorted Janice home. Lester Rudisell kissed Janice good night, and so did Dad! Needless to say, Lester became a thing of the past.

My parents' marriage was the power that supported four headstrong daughters. Their parenting was way ahead of its time, raising us as individuals, not "girls." My dad and mom taught us that we could be anything we desired with hard work and ambition.

They also shared their strong Christian values and taught us to be compassionate and aware of other people's values. They instilled in us the hope, love, and work ethic that is required to make us good contributors to society. We owe them a big debt for their selfless love and sacrifices.

I found out much later in life that our horse-show adventures were made possible because of their sacrifices. My dad would go without lunch all week in order to pay our entry fees at the horse shows. He secretly prayed we would not be so successful at the shows to allow us to be in the running for the High Point trophy.

Much sought-after High Point trophies were offered at the end of the show to the high-scoring horse and rider combination. I was fortunate to win two on a twenty-one-year-old English pleasure pony named Topper. Topper taught me to ride and was an invaluable pony to many young riders. Truly worth his weight in gold.

Mom contributed by sewing our riding habits since we could not afford store bought ones. She also designed the flashy western parade suits, sewing by hand the sequins, rhinestones, and fringe to the pants and vests. She braided numerous ribbons for manes and purchased "tail bows" and glitter, almost on a weekly basis.

We ignorantly disregarded the fact that Mom and Dad were not "horse" people. Neither had any experience with horses, yet they were roped into loading horses, hauling trailers, and handling rowdy ponies before and after classes.

Our passion blinded us to their rapid introduction into the horse-show world. Like most kids, we just assumed our parents knew everything about the world.

I now realize how self-absorbed and immature I became in our pursuit of showing horses. Looking back, I thank God for such innovative and supportive parents.

It was during this time period that I developed my dream to show at a national show. I shared my fantasy with my best friend, Jane. We decided to show at the Madison Square Garden Horse Show. We were going to compete with the best. We planned and tried to become the best rider in our area, figuring it was our first step to reaching our goal.

Often we would take some of Mr. Stroupe's ponies trail-riding. This was like a special retreat from the show ring. We always had to ask for permission from Mr. Stroupe and see who he wanted us to ride. We knew better than to ride our assigned show ponies on trail and were required to ride a horse or pony from his random herd of forty horses and ponies.

Mr. Stroupe was a wise horseman and teacher. He knew it was important to let us learn on our own. He taught us to respect his property and ponies. By requiring us to ask for this special treat, we showed him respect.

Meanwhile, he was benefiting by having his less-experienced ponies trained to trail ride and learn to accept different situations and riders.

As summer was coming to an end, Jane and I decided to enjoy one of our last trail rides. This particular trail ride remains ingrained in my mind. We each rode black ponies, Black Jack and Black Gal, through the forty wooded acres that made up Willow Valley Farms.

We stopped in the woods by a creek to let the ponies graze. As we laid down in a grassy opening, we basked in the beauty of the black ponies silhouetted against the radiant blue sky and char-treuse-green grass and leaves.

Youthful dreams filled our heads, and we could see our future dedicated to horses and our friendship. It was a magical moment in time that will always exist in my memories. It reminds me of my innocence and my appreciation of the world's beauty and all its possibilities. I still treasure that youthful friendship and honest view of the world. Dreams were more than an illusion; they were a plan for the future.

As we matured, Jane and I continued to show horses. We became more and more competitive with each other, causing conflicts in our friendship. This rivalry eventually drove us apart. I became jealous because she seemed to have it all. She was beautiful, had all the best tack and rode the best quality pony owned by Mr. Stroupe. Her dad even bought her a horse trailer.

Meanwhile, I had to share my life with three other horse crazy sisters. We had a limited budget, non quality tack and homemade riding habits. I rode a pretty but less quality pony who had a ton of talent.

Our competitive attitudes soon drove a wedge between us. Judges would place us differently based on their preference of quality or talent. This only intensified the competitiveness. I saw our friendship dissipating but did not know how to stop it.

Eventually, Jane and I ventured down different paths in high school. I worried and watched as her dedication to horses faded away. It hurt me terribly to see her choice of new friends and her loss of equine interest. I saw her drifting away to a harsher side of life, but I was too immature to help her.

I will always remember our good times at Willow Valley Farms. Nowadays, I rarely see her, but when I do, we reflect back on the good times and how our lives took different directions. She had it all and threw it away. Maybe it was good that I had to work so hard for all my achievements. But to this day I wish things could have ended differently. If they had, maybe she would be sharing our dream again and going to a national show.

With the passage of time, some forty years later, I finally reached the possibility to achieve that childhood dream. It was not the Madison Garden show but the American National Welsh Pony Show in Tulsa, Oklahoma. After years of showing at the Welsh shows in our area, Dalton and I decided we were ready for Tulsa.

My devoted husband, Dart, helped me prepare. He was uneasy about us taking the long trip without him. Being a Charlotte firefighter, he had experienced accidents firsthand and had some grim memories that haunted him. Nevertheless, he pursued the possibility of the trip with guarded enthusiasm.

We purchased new tires for the truck and trailer. Dart changed the oil, checked all the hoses, and inspected every part of the truck he could reach. We discussed how to load the feed, hay, and various miscellaneous horse items. Since we had "goose neck trailer," we could not put the hay and items in the back of the truck for fear of possible exposure to rain on the trip out and back. Our dressing room, while spacious, could not accommodate all the hay needed for the trip with two ponies. Eventually we figured it out by using the stallion stall in the front of the horse compartment part of the trailer.

My main concern was money. Most of my adult life had been spent on a shoestring budget. Throwing in a week-long trip to Tulsa with all the expenses and accommodations did not figure into our financial situation. I did not know where we would get the money for this grand adventure.

As the summer wore on into early August, I became despondent, clearly a lack of faith on my part. I entered the show anyway, hoping for a miracle. As my dad often says, "Ask and you shall receive." And receive I did.

God always has a plan, and more often than not, it is not apparent to us. This is where faith enters the picture.

I had no idea that my mom had inherited Exxon stock from her father. True to her character, she just kept reinvesting it all these years after her father's death. Her plan was to leave good financial support to her four daughters.

Unexpectedly, this became known to me after her estate was finally settled later in the summer of 2014. I thought I was beyond crying, but this unexpected last act of selflessness and love had me bawling again. I had more than enough to go to the show and plenty left over for the future. Following her example, I chose to reinvest the remaining stock for our children's future.

I could not believe we were actually going to the WPCSA American National Show! My childhood dream was becoming a reality. God had used a Welsh pony named Rudy to help me step outside my confront zone, handle my fears, and believe in myself and Him.

Since music has always been a comfort and inspiration for me, I started looking for songs that would support me during "future relapses" into insecurity. Music, like art, inspired and comforted me during the preparation period before this big show adventure.

I found tranquility listening to "Tulsa Time" and "Lord, I Hope This Day Is Good," by Don Williams. My strength was renewed while listening to "What a Feeling" from the movie *Flash Dance* and "The Eye of The Tiger" from the movie *Rocky.*

I started concentrating more on my training with Rudy. Nothing was deemed off limits as long as it was safe. I had a plan, and it was followed faithfully. Looking back, I now see the trust we developed in each other during this period of constant pushing the limit.

Rudy, aka Sugar Boy

So we are finally going to the American National Show. I wondered why we were attempting such really crazy things. Some are so outrageous, even for Mel.

She has never let me down, so I cooperated as long as I felt it was reasonable. I know we are the best around here, but I am not sure what we will encounter at the national level, so I understand her persistence in trying difficult maneuvers. Does not really matter to me because I know I am good enough. We will just do the best we can and see what happens.

She and I realize that the human element of horse judging can often fail to produce the correct placings, but I am going to do my best for Mel and Dalton.

Humans are so complicated, and they tend to overthink things. Don't understand why they have to introduce other elements that just don't pertain to judging.

Why do judges care about other people's opinion? Hey, the judge is the judge for a reason. They should just know the rules and make their calls on what happens in the ring. After all, they are the trained professionals.

I hear that the show is in Tulsa, and I'm not sure where that is located. Must be pretty far, as I overheard Mel talking with Dart and Dalton during all the preparations. This may be my biggest adventure yet! I so looking forward to this big show!

Mel

Final preparations for the trip also encompassed the "non equine" part. We had to secure a hotel near the showgrounds, recheck our entries which included countless amounts of paperwork, acquire a map, and find someone to accompany Dalton and me. Dart had to remain at home to work the farm and continue his job as a firefighter.

Luckily, Colten came to the rescue. He volunteered to come along, as well as his girlfriend, Clair. She wanted to see more of America than North Carolina. I could see Dart felt a bit of relief. Similar to myself, Colten is a dreamer. The main difference between us is his better grasp on reality. He handles difficult situations much better than me.

I really admire my son for being such a mature young man. He is a positive, focused individual with unlimited creativity. He is adventurous and willing to devise a plan to achieve his dreams. For example, the day after graduating high school, he set out on a journey of his own with his best friend, Austin. They had established a rock band in middle school and dreamed of making it big in California. With a trailer stocked with all their band equipment accumulated since middle school, they left their parents in a parking lot, moms in tears and dads with concerned looks.

They were successful in arriving in Los Angeles with only a few mishaps, which they handled by themselves. They arranged gigs to play and lived life to the fullest in this exciting, new environment for about nine weeks. Then they experienced some of life's hardships, giving them a reality check. Their struggling to making ends meet without locating a sustainable job being the main one. Their money was running low. They made the decision to return home while they still had enough to get there.

Colten called us while we were vacationing at Holden Beach and let me know they were coming home. I was so heartbroken. These young men had failed at their first attempt in achieving their dream. All the hard work, planning, and envisioning came to a heart-breaking end.

Even so, they kept a sense of humor. After stopping at a Burger King to eat, Colten informed me that they were watching two tornados through the restaurant windows! I could have died with the thought of them in peril, and us thousands of miles away at the beach. He just laughed it off and said they were fine. What a great outlook on life. Wish I could have felt the same way. I knew I would be on pins and needles until they safely arrived home.

We left for Tulsa on a bright, sunny morning in September. Looking at eighteen hours on the road with the ponies never entered my mind. I saw it as a wonderful adventure and a chance to see this spectacular country. We had plenty of snacks, books to read, good music, and companionship. What more did we need?

We played car games, talked endlessly, and took breaks whenever we felt liked eating or letting the ponies off for water and grazing. I loved seeing the variation in scenery and how people lived in other parts of the country. I could hardly wait to see the Mississippi River. That was on my bucket list.

Colten, quite familiar with I-40 after his adventure to California, was well aware of where to stop for gas and the best eating places. On his way home from California, the band decided to reside in Nashville, Tennessee, for a couple years. Although it was country city USA, they believed their brand of old-style rock and roll might find a niche there.

With me knowing nothing about Nashville, Colten gave us a brief tour when we passed through that city, horse trailer and all! He took us by his old apartment complex, the airport, and his place of employment. That was a job he truly hated, but as he noted, "It paid the bills."

Leaving Nashville was a relief. I am always nervous driving a big horse trailer in city traffic. Non-horse people just do not understand that you cannot stop a trailer quickly, especially if it is loaded with horses. They drive like maniacs, trying to get ahead of the horse trailer, even if we are driving above the speed limit. I guess this is just another example of the inconsiderate attitude that has taken over the USA.

Hour after hour passed, and the excitement begin to wane. I wondered what the ponies where thinking, as this was the longest trailer ride they had ever experienced.

Rudy, aka Sugar Boy

Wow. This is absolutely the longest trailer ride I have ever encountered. Where in the world is Tulsa? I was so excited about the possibilities when we started out, but this is a bit much, even for me.

My daughter, Sugar, has accompanied me, and she is really stressing out. She is only two years old and has only been to a few shows. I sure hope Mel checks on her at the next stopped. She is not eating her hay, and that bothers me. I try to comfort her and tell her to look at this as a big adventure, much as my mom told me years ago. I guess I am not as good as my mom with encouragement.

Normally, I love to travel. This is a grand journey for me. We are finally going to the American National Show in Tulsa, Oklahoma. This has been Mel's dream for a long time, and I have to admit, I am a bit excited to be a part of it. But jeez, the drive!

Mel

I thought we would never get through Nashville, Tennessee, alive. Surviving five lane changes on I-40 in five o'clock traffic with a large horse trailer was quite a feat. I thanked God that Colten had come along on this crazy adventure. There was no way I could have navigated this insane engineering disaster on I-40 without him.

*****

Rudy, aka Sugar Boy

Hang on, Sugar. We really don't have any choice on this road. I get a glimpse every now and then, and it looks like a disaster. Relax and keep your feet spread a bit. It will help you with your balance, and you will feel less exhaustion.

I feel so badly for her. She has never been this far from home in her life and definitely not on a trailer for this long. Neither have I, but I don't want to alarm her with that piece of knowledge. I am sure Mel knows that she is doing. At least she has help with Colten and the others.

Mel

Finally, experiencing some open highway after the near disaster in Nashville, we spotted a Cracker Barrel. We managed to enter the tight drive and circled around to the back where there was room to park a large vehicle and trees to provide some shade. We all sighed with relief. We needed the rest and food to energize us.

I gave the nervous ponies their feed and water then headed into the restaurant. We took our time eating, and our fellowship renewed our interest to get back on the road. We rediscussed our plans for the drive straight through to Tulsa, with all agreeing we might need to take a long break at the Mississippi River.

Coming out of the restaurant, I decided to check on the ponies and give them some more hay. I was shocked to see that Sugar had not eaten her grain.

Whenever a horse does not eat, that raises a big red flag. This parking lot was not an appropriate place to unload a possibly sick horse as it was so near the busy high way.

Rudy, aka Sugar Boy

'Bout time you showed up to check us out. I have been worried sick about Sugar. She won't associate with me and refuses to eat. I am sure she is overwhelmed by all the excitement in Nashville. Surely Mel will recognize the problem and fix it. This is one of the few times I wish I could talk.

Mel

Climbing into the truck, I told Colten we needed to stop somewhere quickly so I could unload her off the trailer and see if she would eat some grass. She was showing signs of colic.

I was ignorant about the roads and did not know that after Nashville, you had 197 miles of remoteness before you reached Memphis and the Mississippi.

Mile after mile passed, and night was upon us before we found an exit that had a shopping mall with a parking lot that was suitable. It was isolated, lighted, and had a grassy area behind the stores. A huge, mountainous, natural stone wall bordered the back parking lot. Workers had carved out the side of the mountain to give us this special place to rest and check on Sugar.

I nervously waited to park and unload the ponies. What would I find? I prayed it would not be a situation we could not handle. Critical situations always make people turn to God and pray, and I was no exception.

Rudy, ever the "pig," went right to eating grass. Just another rest stop with grass advantages as far as he was concerned.

Sugar unloaded quietly and stood on the grassy ground with no interest in eating the rich grass. She circled and started to look for a place to lay down. I let her recline and waited to see if she was going to roll, look at her abdomen, or just rest. After a few minutes, she started to roll. We were definitely looking at a case of colic. This was a serious situation, as colic and complications from colic are the number one killer of horses.

Fortunately for me, my oldest sister Ginger is a veterinarian pathologist. She had warned me ahead of time that horses may have colic issues on long drives due to stress. She instructed me to take some BANAMINE, just in case. Wisely, I listened. Pulling out the medication bag, I quickly gave her a shot of BANAMINE. Now all we could do was wait and see if it took effect. This usually takes about fifteen excruciating minutes. It was now late in the evening, and I was so worried. How would we handle this if we needed a vet?

Meanwhile, Dalton bridled Rudy up and rode bareback in the grassy patch next to the mountainous rock wall. We took some great pictures, and I was in awe of the magnificent wall which dwarfed the pair.

As I watched the pair, I soon noticed Sugar nibbling at the grass. Thank God! We let her continue for about thirty minutes. I wanted to see if she would poop before we loaded her back on the trailer.

That would assure me that she did not have a blockage, masked by the pain-relieving BANAMINE. I was never so happy to see a pile of manure and clean it up from the parking lot. We loaded the ponies back on the trailer and I saw Sugar start to eat hay. Relief!

The next 197 miles had us all struggling to stay awake. Colten and I were the only ones talking, and even then, we were trying to stay focused. We passed through town exits like Buck Snort and Toad Lick, chuckling at the names. We stopped for coffee and to refuel, but no more unloading of the ponies.

Finally, we came to the Mississippi River at midnight. Colten woke everyone up to see the big pyramid beside the highway and also the lights on the bridge crossing the river.

Another small problem arose. There was construction on the bridge, and only one lane was open. Traffic was almost at a standstill, and yes, there was a ton of traffic at midnight in Memphis, the town that never sleeps.

I was so relieved that Colten was driving at this time. The only open lane was so narrow due to barrels the 18-wheelers could barely creep through them. I held my breath as Colten navigated the trailer through the narrow space, stopping and starting constantly. My poor ponies! Poor Colten! Later he told me even he was a bit on edge with this situation.

Finally, the end was in sight. I was so grateful. The one thing I really desired to see avoided me. I never got to see the Mississippi River due to the darkness. Colten said that I didn't miss much. It was just a big, muddy river. I was still disappointed, but maybe on the way back home, I would have the opportunity.

We saw a rest station ahead, and we all agreed to stop for about five hours til the sun rose. We were beyond tired and needed to clean up and take a break from all the miles we had covered.

We let the ponies off to drink water and graze on the grass at the back of the parking lot. I cleaned the trailer and made sure the ponies had hay, water, and clean shavings.

After loading them up, Clair, Dalton, and I headed for the bathroom for some refreshing and brushing teeth. We laughed at all the craziness we had encountered along the way and marveled at the wondrous sights we had seen. America was beautiful in all its individual cites, farms, and small towns. I loved seeing how the rest of America lived.

Tired and weary, we all settled into our makeshift beds to attempt sleep. Surely as exhausted as we all were, sleep would come easily. I was in the front seat of the truck, and Dalton was in the back seat. Unfortunately, I could not sleep a wink. I was anxious about the occasional cars coming by in the parking lot. Too many horror stories came to mind from all the true crime stories on TV. Lack of faith kept me from a much-needed rest.

The ponies were anxious too. They kept pawing the trailer and bouncing the truck and trailer around. I prayed they would soon settle down as Colten and Clair were in the large dressing room, experiencing firsthand the constant pounding. We all needed sleep!

Eventually everyone settled down because the next thing I knew, I was awakening at dawn from a restless sleep. Sunrise always inspires me, as if God is saying the world deserves another day to start over.

The rest of the trip was encompassed by amazing scenery, rest stops, and interesting people. We often unloaded the ponies to eat grass, drink, and roll at the well-kept rest stops. The ponies brought laughter and interest from many travelers from not only the USA but also Canada and foreign countries.

"Not knowing a stranger," I often talked with many of the curious travelers and introduced them to the Welsh pony breed. I was sometimes surprised to find many had a Welsh pony story to share. Seems these beloved, though mischievous, ponies have quite the influence in the equestrian world.

I loved seeing the country and meeting many new people. I acknowledged this would be a trip to remember regardless of the show results.

Chapter 7

Life's a dance. You learn as you go. Sometimes you lead, sometimes you follow. Don't worry about what you don't know. Life's a dance. You learn as you go.

—John Michael Montgomery

When I first entertained the idea of the national show in Tulsa, I secretly hoped we might win a national championship. My teenage dream emerged into my fifty-something-year-old body to allow the chance that the impossible just might be possible. I finally realized just how good Rudy, Dalton, and I really were.

I also recognized the fact that we had no idea about the competition, show trends, or our lack of identity in the Welsh pony community. We were "unknown" to the national Welsh show community and well-established farms.

My old insecurities started to creep into my mind: the fear of the unknown, the fear of failure, and the fear of…maybe just not being good enough. Was I just a dreamer and not a doer? Did I have the faith to believe in Dalton, Rudy, and myself? Only time would tell, and we were about to find out just where we stood.

Arriving in Tulsa was quite an eye-opener. Traffic was heavy, and we did not have a clear idea of where the show facility was or what it looked like. We were so ready for this journey to end. Finally, our destination appeared in sight. Exhausted from the journey, I still managed to achieve some excitement as we pulled into gate number 7. It was just past six in the evening, and I was totally ignorant about where to go other than gate number 7. The facility was enormous and intimidating.

I did not know where to unload the ponies, where our stalls were, or who to ask about our stabling. Everyone in our truck looked to me for the answers. God has a way of helping those who need solutions. The gate crew came to our rescue and showed us where to park, the procedure to unload, and where the show office was located, as well as the Welsh pony stabling.

Rudy, aka Sugar Boy

Thank God. I have arrived! So this is Tulsa. Pretty busy place. Look, Sugar. What a fancy place. Can't wait til I am off this trailer. Hope the stalls are as nice as the rest of this facility. Wonder who our stable neighbors will be?

Mel

We all begin the process of settling the ponies into their stalls, unpacking everything we would need for the show, and cleaning the trailer.

Rudy came off the trailer, his old confident self with only a curious interest in the chaotic activity. He just wanted to settle into his stall and have his supper. He was so stoic and practically ignored all the commotion. Sugar was wide-eyed, but followed his example and settled quickly into her stall beside him.

Once everything was completed, I left the others to retrieve our show pack. The show office was located in a trailer right beside gate number 7. I noticed the gate officials still scurrying to keep the lanes of traffic open.

Exhausted from the journey and sleep-deprived, I completely overlooked the handwritten sign which read, "Closed @ 7 p.m." I knocked on the door, surprised that it was locked. Seconds later, the door flew open with a bang, and a large, angry man came out screaming at me.

"Can you not read?" the show manager yelled rudely. "We closed at seven!"

I was so shocked I could only stammer that I had missed the handwritten sign he now directed my eyes to read. Stunned, I quietly apologized for missing the sign, explaining that the eighteen-hour drive from North Carolina had me in a sleep-deprived daze.

"Come back tomorrow morning," he squawked as he slammed the door in my face.

Stupefied for a moment, my anger quickly overrode my astonishment at this altercation. I stomped back to the horse trailer where everyone was patiently waiting to drop the trailer and find the hotel.

Not one to hide my quick temper, it was apparent that I was really upset as I approached the gathering at the trailer. Explaining what an "ass" the show manager was sent my son Colten into action. He headed out toward the to show office to confront the manager for being so rude to his mom. Not the reaction I wanted. We were so new to this area, and I had already upset one show official. I did not need to incite any backlash.

I finally persuaded him not to get involved, reminding him that we still needed to move the trailer and locate the trailer parking lot. No time for retribution. I needed to think this thing through when I was not irate.

As usual, when you are tired and upset, nothing is easy. Once again, the gate workers assisted us in parking our trailer. Because of the lack of parking space in the fair area, they instructed us to pull back out of the gate and go about a half mile down the road. Not only was this an inconvenience, it also meant we had to reassure we had everything we needed for the show and also unload all our luggage for our stay at the hotel. No one was in the mood to do all this extra work.

Leaving the fairgrounds was a fiasco, with trailers pulling in and out and traffic from locals getting off work. We had trouble navigating the two lanes of traffic while searching for the parking lot.

Eventually, we located the trailer parking lot on the right and went through the "check-in" process. Once that was completed, we were assigned a spot in what looked like hundreds of trailers. They were packed so close together I was scared to back the trailer into our assigned small piece of "real estate." Colten offered to back the trailer, and everyone helped him navigate the close quarters.

After unloading our personal gear, we now had to locate the hotel and hoped that our cell phone with directions would not send us on a wild goose chase. Exhausted and disillusioned, I begin to question my decision to come to Tulsa. Clair encouraged me by saying she had enjoyed the trip so far, and the best was yet to come. After all, we had the fair to look forward to as well as the Welsh pony show. I found her to be an eternally optimistic person and was grateful she came with us.

Wednesday morning found me enjoying a good breakfast and leaving the hotel alone. It was seven, and being the worrier of the group, I wanted to make sure the ponies stayed on their same feeding routine.

As I entered gate number 7, I was sure the ponies were stressed and probably sleep-deprived. I could envision them waiting patiently in their stalls, wondering about their morning feed. Approaching their stalls, I was relieved to hear their eager nickering and see their bright eyes.

The morning activities were just as busy as the previous evening. Adults and children scurried everywhere in the barn aisles, dragging hay nets, water hoses, and grain buckets. I felt right at home in this early morning show scenario.

Once the ponies were fed and stalls cleaned, I headed back to the hotel. I quickly found myself confused in my surroundings. All the roads looked alike to me, and I could not find any landmarks that looked familiar.

When I saw the University of Tulsa, I knew for sure I was lost and turned into the entrance to turn around. Luckily, I found a student who gave me directions to our hotel. I sure wasn't going to let Colten and Dalton know that I had lost my way. Not only would they never let me live it down, they would further humiliate me by never letting me drive alone.

Entering the hotel, I found everyone up and ready to eat breakfast, so I enjoyed a second breakfast with them. You never know at a horse show when or if you will have another meal that day.

Arriving at the showgrounds, the place was bustling with activity. Trailers were arriving with all kinds of livestock and vendors for the fair. It would be busy all day on Wednesday, as the actual fair opening day was Thursday.

Colten, Clair, and Dalton headed to the stalls while I ventured to the show office. As I entered the slightly crowded office, I saw two officials, each working with a line of exhibitors. Wouldn't you know it. My line, the "A thru M" exhibitors, was where the rude show manager sat. I dreaded the upcoming confrontation.

Gradually, I worked my way forward. I had to admit, I was pretty impressed with the efficiency of the show officials. When I approached "ole grumpy" for my show packet, he did not even look up as I told him my name. He had to look up as he handed my show pack to me. What happened next took me totally by surprise.

He actually apologized to me for his rude behavior the previous evening.

He explained that he had been working pretty much 24-7 to get the grounds ready for this special event. He was in charge of the whole fair, not just the Welsh pony show. I smiled and thanked him for his apology. I reassured him that all was forgiven, and I turned to leave. I was so relieved. I hate confrontation, and by the grace of God, this one eventually turned out to making a new friend. I planned to visit him again later when I had some spare time.

Shows are extremely stressful once they commence. Wednesday was going to be a day for exploring and locating bathrooms, Welsh Pony Show office, eating establishments, wash pits, and entrances to the rings.

Sugar would be showing in the Wednesday afternoon halter classes, so we wanted to have time to get both ponies in all the arenas. Indoor rings can be spooky, and Dalton wanted to inspect the arenas for any problem areas. She decided to ride Rudy first and quickly saddled up. I brought Sugar along to lunge her and let her inspect the arenas as well.

Saddled up, we headed to the ring with Rudy and Sugar observing all the exciting activity firsthand. Numerous ponies were working out last-minute problems or executing last minute changes. Trainers and show moms were constantly yelling instructions while their riders strained to attempt the maneuvers and hear the directions over all the activities and noise.

True to form, Rudy looked at everything with interest, but was not overly alarmed at anything. Dalton was nervous, but very focused on achieving a good ride and keeping Rudy focused.

As I watched from the entrance gate, I notice a nicely dressed cowboy standing down at the other end of the gate. He must be a real Oklahoma cowboy! Since Dart used to rodeo, I wanted to strike up a conversation with the Oklahoma cowboy.

Pleasantly, I introduced myself with a quick hello. He curtly replied with a hello then looked back at the arena. I took the hint that he was not interested in a conversation. Boy, was everyone in Tulsa so unfriendly?

Dalton rode over to the gate and asked me what I thought about Rudy's performance. I told her he looked good, so we proceeded back to the stalls. After untacking Rudy, my full attention now turned to Sugar, who had to be washed and readied for the afternoon classes.

Dalton and Colten quickly volunteered, as they knew I needed to locate a leather lead. I assumed they had a tack vendor set up somewhere in the facilities, so I set out on my own.

While the others headed for the wash pits, I went to the Welsh pony information booth in the barn to inquire about a tack vendor. Every large show I have attended usually had tack vendors, so I assumed the American National Show would surely have one on the grounds.

I approached the two ladies working the WPCSA booth and asked about a tack vendor. They quickly told me there were no equine tack vendors anywhere on the Tulsa State Fair grounds. I almost had a panic attack while thinking about trying to locate a tack store in

Tulsa. We were getting close on time, and I did not need another distraction to put a kink in our plans.

One of the ladies asked what I needed. After explaining that I required a leather lead, she requested that I accompany her to our stalls and show her my pony and my available tack. Looking through my options, she quickly picked out a bridle that she thought was best for this particular class and the age of the pony. She suggested that I attach the lead to the noseband of this particular bridle since the pony had never had a bit in her mouth. She also told me to put the bridle on her without reins then leave her in the stall and let her eat hay. That way she would become accustomed to the bit.

With a sheepish grin, I reminded her that the lead was the reason I had inquired about a tack vendor. Oh yeah. I could see she had an "Oh, I got offtrack" moment. She promptly escorted me to her stalls where she pulled out a leather lead that perfectly matched my bridle. The only request was to return it that afternoon after I had shown Sugar.

I was astonished that a total stranger would offer to do this for another competitor. I graciously thanked her and promised that I would return it promptly after my class.

Experiencing mostly amiable exhibitors at all the previous regional Welsh shows, why was I so astonished to see the same charity at the National level? The Welsh exhibitors are truly hospitable competitors. They want to win, but not because you lacked the correct attire or tack. They want to win because they had the better pony that day, fair and square! What a difference from the competitors from my former breed association.

Time came around for us to tack up and head to the arena for Sugar's halter class. As we waited for the officials to arrive, I glanced around at our competition. Some of the mares were spectacular. I knew we were not going to beat them, but I felt like we should place in the top three or four.

Finally, the officials arrived, and the class began. I watched as one by one the ponies were called into the arena to trot past the judges then stand for inspection.

When our turn came, Sugar exhibited beautifully, trotting into the ring with a presence and grace that surprised even me. Too bad we entered when the judges had their back to us. The gate keeper sent us in too soon, and both judges were still studying the previous pony.

I was so embarrassed and had to reenter the arena. I could just envision the judges saying, "What a rookie." We placed a dismal fifth, and I am sure our early entrance played a part in our placing.

Being a certified judge myself, I felt Sugar should have placed in the top three. I was a bit frustrated at the gate keeper's lack of clarity on our entrance. We appeared amateurish at the biggest show of our life. I could have kicked myself for not paying attention to the judges. Totally my fault. Even so, I had several spectators approached me after the class. They asked about her breeding and told me she was beautiful young pony.

After the Wednesday showing, we were free until the Friday afternoon show. Rudy and I would be showing in the A and B adult Western pleasure classes. I was confident we would at least win a ribbon, but secretly I hoped for much more.

We visited the fair on Thursday, worked Rudy in the rings during the lunch breaks, and let Sugar graze on any grass I could find. I wanted her to enjoy showing and felt this grazing would put things more in perspective for her.

After returning Sugar to her stall, I set out to explore more of the arenas, food vendors, as well as the Welsh pony registry publicity area. It was there I noticed a silent auction set up, with many articles of clothing, books, and miscellaneous Welsh items. It was benefiting the WPCSA, so I decided to contribute to the cause.

Along with all the show and feeding supplies, I had also brought along some screen-printed T-shirts that I had designed. They corresponded with the previous magazine article that Danny and Mariah had helped me write, "Welsh, Not Just for Kids."

As I was picking out a size that would be appropriate for the auction, I also decided to make a goodwill gesture to the Tulsa State Fair show manager. After all, I had called him an "ass," even though he did not know. He had apologized, and I felt this would make up for my verbal outburst, even if he did not hear it.

I was relieved to find the show office empty except for him and another female official. He looked up apprehensively as I entered the door.

Approaching him, I handed him the Welsh T-shirt and explained that I wanted him to have it. I hoped he would keep it as a reminder of the woman who came all the way from North Carolina with her Welsh ponies to show in Tulsa. He was shocked. He stood up and introduced himself as Larry Brown. He also told me that in all the years of managing the show facility, no one had ever given him anything. Even though it was a Welsh pony shirt, he was grateful to receive it. He thanked me with sincere enthusiasm. He told me he was going to hang it in his band room.

Did I just hear "band room?"

This led to a conversation on rock music and a growing friendship. I told him about Colten's band and listened to his band's history. We became fast friends with this common connection. I could not wait to tell Colten all about Larry Brown's band and my reconciliation with him.

This friendship would last through to the future Tulsa shows, whenever we were able to attend. I always paid a visit to the show office and was pleased to see that Larry remembered the lady from North Carolina despite all the thousands of people he encountered each year.

In 2015, when I entered the show office, the first thing Larry said was, "Well, you did come back!"

Friday morning had us headed to the showgrounds with a growing appreciation for the number 7 gatekeepers. They were always friendly and courteous every time we entered or exited. Maybe this was how the genuine Oklahoma folks behaved.

On Friday morning, the weather was cool. We decided to take them coffee and biscuits from McDonalds. I guessed at what they wanted and hoped it would be adequate. This gesture surprised them, and they eagerly accepted the handout. Little did I know that this was the start of another friendship that would continue into future American National Welsh Pony shows.

After tending to the ponies, we all headed to the main arena to watch the morning show which consisted of the purebred Welsh halter classes. Sitting there, Dalton and I each placed and discussed the classes as we saw them. Most of the time we agreed with the judges' placings. This assured me that we at least had some judges that appeared to be impartial.

In came a class of nineteen section C/D Welsh cob mares. The D cobs are the largest of the breed sections of Welsh ponies. They can even be "horse" size with no limitation on their heights. They are stately and beautiful with flowing manes, thick tails, and feathering on their lower legs. The C's are a smaller version and just as beautiful.

Being a judge, I always take notice of not only the horse but also the trend in the exhibitor's clothing. I noticed a young woman with a "funky-looking" outfit—pretty, but not what I would consider as proper attire for showing. It did catch my attention, and I immediately picked her beautiful mare as my first-place choice.

Dalton agreed with me as this exhibitor made her way around the arena. Eventually the young woman stood her mare up right in front of us, where I got a closer look at the mare and the outfit the handler was wearing.

Colten surprisingly exclaimed, "That's Miranda Lambert!"

"No way," I blurted out as I looked at the show program. As I searched for the exhibitor's number, I laughed at Colten's insistence that it was indeed Miranda Lambert. All I could recover from the program was the owner of the mare was Sheldon, which meant nothing to me. That could have been a farm or ranch name.

"I am not kidding!" he excitedly replied with big eyes.

Before I could reply, the woman sitting next to him said, "Sure is. She owns that Welsh cob mare."

Did I hear that correctly? I could not believe the famous country singer was here in Tulsa, showing a Welsh cob. Boy, was I in high cotton now! I could not wait to call Dart and tell him.

Our first pick, Miranda's mare, went reserve champion. Dalton and I both thought she should have gone champion but were satisfied to see her place reserve champion in such a nice big class.

We decided to stay for a few more classes. Colten and Clair left us to try and find the closest restrooms and pick up a few snacks. When they returned, Colten told me Miranda had talked to him. Since Colten was a musician, I was eager to hear what she had said. Maybe she had given him some advice for promoting his band. What a great opportunity for him!

Standing by the restroom door, Colten heard, "Excuse me," as Miranda entered the women's room.

He laughed so hard at me for thinking they had carried on a serious music discussion.

"Real funny, Colten," I replied, rolling my eyes.

"I think it is time we head to the stalls to get ready for my western classes. We have an hour lunch break, and then we have my first performance class."

Chapter 8

Champions believe in themselves when no one else does.

—"Heart of a Champion"

It is difficult to imagine all the emotions you feel when you are about to achieve the one thing you have pursued for most of your life. The time was at hand, and I would attain the goal I had set so many years ago. This was not just a minor goal but a force that had directed me in almost every aspect of my life. Even if I did not understand my destination, I could now reflect and see how it had kept me motivate to pursue my dream. Only God knew where it would lead.

The journey to this moment had taught me many of life lessons. Using a Welsh pony, God had taught me to believe in myself, to accept life's disappointments as a growing process, to rejoice in the victories, and to continue on the path that He had set before me. This amazing journey to accept myself for who I am began with a wonderful Welsh pony named Rudy.

Rudy led me to take a closer look at life, my relationship with God, and other people in the world. He taught me to believe in myself, regardless of other's opinions. I had made it to Tulsa. Now it was "showtime!"

As Dalton and Colten prepared Rudy, I left to go change into my show clothes in the ladies' restrooms. With plenty of mirrors and changing stalls, I could take my time without interfering with the other competitors. I also wanted a place where I could pray for a safe ride and the confidence to do my best. I needed the time alone to meditate and calm my nerves.

Arriving back at the stalls, I found Rudy tacked up and ready to go. Colten helped me mount up, and I headed toward the warm-up area. This is it! I prayed our ride to the arena would be uneventful.

The warm-up area was packed, and I scrutinized the other ponies. I was looking for possible problem ponies and the ones that were well trained. This helped me prepare for how I would position myself on the rail. It also gave me time to compare Rudy to the other ponies. They were all new exhibitors to me.

Viewing all the gorgeous ponies, hopeful riders, and anxious owners, I tried to relish every moment. I was really here. I recalled the verses from the song, Irene Cara's "What a Feeling."

"What a feeling… I can have it all, now I'm dancing (riding) for my life… Take your passion and make it happen." I had the passion, and I was going to do my best to make it happen. Champions have to believe in themselves, even if no one else does! I believed in Sugar Boy, and he believed in himself and me.

As I entered the arena in the first of the three Western pleasure classes, I could barely control all my emotions. This was it.

The first class was conformation Western pleasure. Although a performance class, this class puts a little more emphasis on the build of the pony or horse. The pony should have the correct conformation to exhibit the proper gaits for a Western pony.

I scanned the arena to find my special place that was far away from any problem ponies and where I could be visible to the judge. The ring was packed, so this was going take a skilled pony and rider. No daydreaming on this trip. I must stay focused. Rudy was "spot on" in this class and responded like the champion I knew he was. I settled into the ride with optimism. Rudy remained alert, but confident and steady.

When we were called into the lineup, I felt satisfied with our performance. As we waited in the lineup for the placings, I hoped for a ribbon…no, really, for a top three ribbon. I was ecstatic when they called Blueridge Rising Star out for second place! He was in the running for the championship!

Patting his neck, I said, "Keep up the good work, Rue!"

We were back on the rail for the working Western pleasure class. This class required a well-trained pony because the judge could call for any kind of maneuver. I was secure in Rudy's training and secretly hoped they would give us a small test. Needless to say, the judge ran the usual class specs with no special maneuvers.

This time we placed third. This positioned us in reserve championship at this point. One more class. If we placed first or second, we would get the reserve!

Back on the rail in the Western pleasure stakes class, the one with the money! I could really use the money!

Everything was going beautifully. Rudy was steady, I was confident, and so far, we had stayed out of trouble.

I glanced around and saw a palomino mare quickly approaching us in the corner. She was one of the ponies I had tried to avoid as she had been misbehaving in the other two classes. The rider had her hands full and was struggling to keep the mare near the center of the ring, away from the other competitors on the rail. I had thus far been successful in my attempt to keep my distance from her.

The announcer called for the lope, and Rudy was right on cue, almost like he was listening to the announcer.

As we approached the straight away in the ring, the palomino mare swerve directly into Rudy, bucking and kicking out at him. In self-defense he bolted forward in an attempt to distance himself from the irate mare.

Just my luck, Rudy farted extremely loud as he scrambled to get out of the way. I was looking at the judge, who previously had her back to us. After the loud expulsion of gas, the judge quickly turned around and saw both ponies bolting forward.

The announcer quickly called for a walk so everyone could regain control. I was so proud of Rudy as he transitioned to a halt and quietly stood until everyone had settled. I was also pissed at the mare that had interfered with Rudy.

The judge then called for a reverse and continued the class. I was heartbroken since the judge did not see the whole incident. Rudy had been the perfect gentleman and only tried to save himself from injury. The championships were definitely lost. I might not even place.

I was surprised when we placed third and upset that this mare had just caused us the reserve championship. My dream crumbled, but I still believed that Rudy was the best in the ring. We had placed in all our classes and had given an honest effort. Life just threw us a curve.

As we untacked, a woman approached our stalls. She had spoken to me earlier and was actually one of the first exhibitors to introduce herself. Her name was Tammy, and I learned that she was from California. I quickly discovered that she attended this show annually and was quite knowledgeable about the Welsh pony. Every year she drives four days to get to Tulsa, often alone with only her ponies and dogs. I admired her dedication.

After greeting me, she gave me some advice about the Western pleasure classes. She loved Rudy, but told me his jog was way to slow and the reins were way to slack. They liked a more-collected headset and a faster jog, similar to the Arabian Western horses. Too bad I did not know this before the classes. In that respect, I acknowledged my ignorance had also played a part in our placings. Rudy was capable of the exact changes she had suggested. I just did not research enough to ride him the correct way for the Welsh pony.

We were through for the day. I would be showing the next day at 7:30 a.m. in the adult trail class. This would be my last class before turning it over to Dalton for the classic Welsh Ridden and adult English pleasure classes on Saturday afternoon.

We decided to visit the Tulsa State Fair again and had a great time. We learned about Belgian Blue cattle, which none of us had ever seen. They are the "Arnold Schwarzenegger" of the beef cattle world. I could not believe these cows were not on steroids.

We visited the many vendors and saw beautiful art, jewelry, and leather works. I saw some similarities but many differences from the North Carolina State Fair.

After a busy and successful day, we decided to search for a good restaurant. No fast food. Colten used his phone to find one of the best Italian restaurants I have ever had the pleasure of visiting. We had a delight fun meal and good service.

Things were looking up! I just had to worry about my 7:30 appointment for the trail class. So early in the morning! 5:30 a.m. came quickly. I needed to eat breakfast and leave for the showgrounds no later than 6:15. Dalton was going to accompany me and help feed the ponies and prepare Rudy for the trail class. Colten and Clair opted to sleep and prepare for the long ride home. We would pick them up after the trail class so they could watch Dalton ride.

I was a bit nervous as I did not know the pattern at this point and had no idea what to expect at the national level. We had only one defeat in trail at the local level.

That defeat happened on a windy, cloudy day. Wind plays havoc with horses' minds. The trail class was held in a pasture where the terrain was wet and rough. I was not too worried, and Rudy appeared calm. Everything was going well, then Rudy missed a canter lead.

The surprised winner swore that I did it on purpose as this was something simple to execute, and Rudy never missed leads. Looking back, I think it was to humble me and prepare me for our trip to the nationals. After all, you learn more from your mistakes than your successes.

After picking up a copy of the trail pattern, Dalton and I arrived at the arena right on time. I learned that we could ride our pattern at any time. There was no set order of go. Learning this, I handed Rudy over to Dalton and climbed into the bleachers to watch some of the other ponies on course. This would help me memorize the pattern and see what was most problematic for the ponies.

As I watched and mentally rode the pattern, I recognized what was going to be my nemesis. This structure had an eight- or nine-foot PVC pipe placed with each end on the top of a round white plastic barrel. The rider was to ride up to either barrel, pick up the end of the pipe, and ride a complete circle without the other end falling off the barrel or the rider dropping the pipe.

Wow. In my opinion, this was the most difficult obstacle on the course. I had never attempted anything like that.

As I was riding it over and over in my mind, a mother and her young daughter came and sat beside me. I heard the mother trying to encourage and comfort her anxious child. The young girl was so scared to show in the trail class. I could not help but feel compassion for this young exhibitor. I also sympathized with her mother's attempt to instill confidence in her. I had firsthand experience through Dalton and my bad show episodes with Rudy.

I struck up a conversation and told the young girl that all she had to do was to believe in her pony and herself. If she did not succeed, then have fun trying. Sympathizing with her, I confessed that I was nervous as well.

"Just ride the pattern in your mind until you feel like you are ready," I told her. "I will wish you good luck, and I just know you will do your best." As I left to find Dalton and Rudy, I hoped that I had helped her out.

I quickly relieved Dalton of holding Rudy, who can be a "busybody" when left alone too long. As she helped me mount up, I prayed that we would give a good showing.

In my mind I told myself, "If I can just get by the barrel obstacle, I will be okay."

Riding into the chute, I knew it was my go next. *Please don't let me forget the pattern*, I prayed. I was a nervous wreck. All the what-ifs played over in my mind.

Sitting there on Rudy, I was amazed at what happened next. Literally Rudy looked around at me, directly into my eyes. If he could have talked, this is what he would have said: *"I got this", he told me with confidence.*

With that said, he turned his attention back to the pony on course in the arena. I was sure he was going to handle this, and I decided that I was going to do my part as well. That was the clearest he had ever communicated to me. I felt empowered and instantly at ease.

I waited patiently for the previous pony to clear the arena. As we rode into the arena, I looked around to plan my trip. I stopped and looked up at the announcer stand, waiting for the judge to acknowledge me to go. A quick nod, and we were on our way.

We handled the first two obstacles with no problems. By the third obstacle, I was feeling pretty confident. This obstacle required the riders to approach a bucket, pick up a branding iron with fluorescent paint, and ride over to a real cowhide thrown over a sawhorse. After branding the cow, you rode back to the bucket and replaced the branding iron.

I decided that since they did not instruct you on how to return the iron that I would show off a bit. Instead of walking it back to the bucket, I decided to back to the bucket and replace the iron. Rudy backed beautifully and stood motionless as I returned the iron to the bucket. I hoped it would give us some extra points.

We had the barrels next. That would be our downfall if we had one. So far, no one had achieved it successfully.

I rode straight to the first barrel, where I could pick up the pipe with my right hand. Stopping Rudy by the barrel, I slowly reached down and picked up the end of the pipe. He stood quietly. I knew I would have to watch the other end of the pipe to ensure it did not move as we circled around the second barrel. I could not watch the pony's head or direction. I had to feel where he was going as I watched the end of the pipe.

It was a true test of trust between the rider and pony. Any deviation of speed or direction would cause the rider to lose balance or drop the other end. Looks simple, but actually, it is very complicated.

Our communication was perfect, and Rudy responded to my hands, seat, legs, and neck reining. We aced it! Our circle was perfect, and the end of the pipe never deviated off the center of the barrel.

I gave a sigh of relief. The hardest part of the pattern was behind us, and our confidence increased with each new obstacle. I was actually enjoying the class. As we crossed the bridge, which was the last obstacle, I almost burst with joy. We had the ultimate show of communication between horse and rider.

Dalton ran up and greeted us with a big smile as we left the arena.

"That was perfect!" she exclaimed.

It was the first time I had heard such a grand response from her. It was a joy to see her so excited.

We took Rudy back to the stalls to untack and give him a well-earned and seldom offered treat. He eagerly accepted the gift then went to munching his hay.

I headed back to the arena to see if there were any more rides. As I approached the stands, I saw the "Oklahoma cowboy" judge leaving the arena accompanied by the show steward. Was I surprised!

"Nice ride. Now, you know why I did not converse with you the other day." The steward quickly urged him on his way.

Wow.

Now I needed to head to the Welsh show office and see how we placed. I wanted this so badly but feared we would fall short of the blue. I had not seen all the rides. Much to my surprise, I won the class! I knew we had a superb ride, but I never know how the judge will call it. At least in trail, you have the advantage of tests that reveal your skill and training level.

Rudy had won his first national championship! We had bragging rights! I was ecstatic!

It was time for the lunch break. After retrieving my blue ribbon, I headed back to the stalls. I could not wait to display it on our tack room wall. Dalton reminded me that we also had to pick up Colten and Clair so that they could watch her in the English classes.

After lunch and retrieving Colten and Clair, we all pitched in to prepare Rudy and Dalton for the classic Welsh ridden and the adult English pleasure classes.

These classes were very competitive, so we needed to braid Rudy's extravagantly long thirty-six-inch mane. While it was beautiful in the Western classes, it was a big pain in the ass to braid for the English classes. Dalton and I spent a couple of hours braiding and re-braiding, arguing constantly about how it looked. Dalton is a perfectionist, and she had to have it perfect. Tension was at an all-time high, and Colten had to rein us in as we fussed over the mane.

Dalton argued, "Why don't you just pull the mane like the rest of the Welsh ponies? You know this is a lot more trouble than it is worth."

I guess my artistic instinct had a part in the decision to grow this long mane. Rudy had the ability to grow a long mane and fore-lock, so why not use that distinction to make him more recognizable and memorable? In fact, at our regional shows, Rudy became known as the "Fabio" of the pony world. His luxurious mane brought him attention from spectators and exhibitors from other breeds. He even developed a fan club. We constantly had children come to our trailer while we were unloading, eagerly asking if we brought Rudy to the show. So I argued back that there was a reason for my eccentric ways. I just wanted her to shut up and quit griping about his mane.

Eventually, we succeeded in braiding the massive mane. Dalton was no longer stressed, but extremely angry. I guess that was a better mood for her as long as the anger was directed toward me and not Rudy.

Making our way to the arena, I tried to give Dalton some suggestions, which she really didn't need or hear. I have to give her credit. She is very professional in the show ring, even when Rudy is not quite perfect. She is so smooth at making their performance look flawless.

Every time she enters the ring, I am always reminded of the "show from hell." Rudy is pretty trustworthy, but he is still a young stallion. I prayed we would not see that unpredictable side today. Welsh are notorious for being spontaneously naughty.

Watching from the ringside, I feel like I have to ride every stride with her to ensure his good behavior. After all, Rudy and I have this special connection. I can feel and see what he is thinking, and sometimes that worries me.

Meanwhile, Dalton tends to be all business and not into the "relationship" concept. This only encourages Rudy to take advantage of her when she least expects it. He is a Welsh after all, and they can be disobedient just for the sake of it. Most owners and riders soon learn you must have a good sense of humor to work with them.

The first class for Rudy and Dalton was the Classic Welsh Ridden. There were nineteen entries. This is probably the most significant class for the Welsh pony to win. It embodies everything the Welsh pony should encompass: conformation, true gaits, athletic ability, discipline, and exhilarating energy.

Rudy, aka Sugar Boy

Well, I guess it's Dalton's turn. Mel and I really had a good time in the trail and Western classes. In trail, she actually read my mind and took my advice. I could feel her relaxing as we went on course.

After watching all the other ponies, I knew the pattern inside and out. She just had to trust me. That is all I have ever wanted—her full attention and trust.

I have enjoyed this show thus far. I love all the activity and seeing some really nice ladies. I still think we should have won the Western championship.

I overheard a lady critiquing our performance…after the fact. We would have won it if I had known this information beforehand.

Oops. Need to quit daydreaming and get back to the work at hand. Dalton is ready to warm up, and she is in her "all business" mood. Just wish she knew how much I hate these braids. If she could feel how much it pulls my mane and itches. Ah, the unnecessary torments of the show pony.

Gate is opening. Time to go. Showtime! Break a leg, Dalton! I got that saying from watching TV last summer through Mel and Dart's bedroom window.

Mel

I held my breath as Rudy entered the ring. I really wanted us to have a good showing, not just for Rudy but for Dalton as well. She had a hard time this year and needed a good boost in her morale. Dalton is a very accomplished rider. I feel she does not receive the recognition she deserves. Her talent is way beyond her years, and her communication skills are a gift from God.

Glancing at the in gate, I could see that Dalton had her hands full with all the excited ponies. The energy generated to supply the ponies with the presence needed to win this class, filled the arena. Even with all the excitement, Rudy was exhibiting the discipline required and was responding well to Dalton's cues.

I noticed a palomino stallion with an extraordinary trot. In my opinion, he was the clear winner unless he had a serious mistake. Rudy should be a close second.

When they asked for the canter, the palomino made a serious mistake. He missed his lead and bolted out of control, giving his rider a challenging ride. Both ways of the ring this pony displayed incredible talent and a clear lack of control.

After the rail work, the ponies were brought in, and the "grooms" or assistants came out to help strip the ponies of their saddles so the judge could view their conformation.

I rushed out to assist Dalton with Rudy. Keeping a stallion quiet for this long period of judging was not an easy accomplishment. Although the lineup was little bit "rowdy," Rudy behaved. Once this was completed, the ponies were resaddled to complete an individual riding pattern before the final placings could be established.

I watched intently as Rudy approached the start of the pattern. I could sense some hesitation on Dalton's part and knew she felt a lack of confidence in Rudy for whatever reason.

On pattern as she approached the diagonal line where you exhibited the extended trot, I grew anxious. This gait was one of Rudy's strong points and could move him to the top if he performed it perfectly. Midway through the line, he broke gait into the canter for about three strides. Not good and definitely a game changer. I could see Dalton was upset, but she rode the rest of the pattern conservatively with no problem.

When the placings were made, the Palomino won, even with his major mistakes and unruly personality. Rudy placed fourth. I was discontented with the placings but congratulated Dalton on her professionalism and her ability to make Rudy's performance look easy.

We headed back to the stalls and recognized we only had time for a quick lunch and a brief rest before the English pleasure division. Rudy had to be re-braided, washed, and ready to go by the end of the lunch break.

I was looking forward to these classes as they were our last chance to win another championship. After that we could start preparations for heading home.

Once we packed, hooked up and loaded the trailer, we could start our journey. Going home was looking better and better. I longed to see Dart, North Carolina, and the farm.

We all worked together during the lunch break and achieved the impossible task of eating, washing Rudy and re-braiding his impossibly long, thick mane. Even Clair helped with the braiding. She had learned so much at this one horse show, and we discovered she was very good at braiding.

When we heard the call for the show to start, we were prepared but anxious to get to the ring. Dalton had her old confidence back and was enthused to show in these classes. Watching them enter the ring, I was relieved to see the harmony was back between Rudy and Dalton.

As I watched their performance, I hardly noticed any other pony. I was mesmerized by Dalton and Rudy's professional performance. Rudy was spectacular, and his gaits were fluid and free. He was soft on the bit and round all the way through his body. Even with his natural talent, it took a special rider to bring forth all his quality. They looked effortless as they proceeded around the crowded arena.

As they called for the lineup, I knew the first class went well. Rudy placed second in the conformation English Pleasure. Dalton was smiling. I gave a great sigh of relief. For once, we were all happy. We were in the running for the championship.

In the working phase, Rudy and Dalton won the class! I could hardly contain my enthusiasm. We were tied for the championship! Could this really be happening? Colten and Clair were clapping and cheering.

For some unknown reason, Rudy dropped down to third in the stakes class. We lost the championship with this placing. Were we going to lose the reserve again? I anxiously awaited the results.

When I heard Blueridge Rising Star as reserve champion, it was amazing. We had arrived at the nationals with the hope of placing. I could not believe we had won a championship and a reserve championship.

We had done it. With the help of all my family and friends, we had achieved the impossible dream. I thanked God and everyone involved. What a feeling...just to be there. We had it all!

I knew this would be a trip that I would relive the rest of my life. Each moment was special and embedded in my heart and mind. What a feeling. For a moment, all the world was right. You can have it all. To God be the glory!

Chapter 9

Coincidences are just God's way of staying anonymous.

—Albert Einstein

The final chapter in this book is the real reason I wanted to share Rudy and my adventure. Every time I tell this story to friends or strangers, I get the same response—a true show of amazement in their eyes and a big "Wow!"

I hope sharing our story with strangers and friends will open eyes to see the wonderful possibilities that God has in store for each individual. I want to encourage people to search out, on their own, God's handy work in even the most minute situations. I want you to recognize the miracles that happen every day. Nothing in this world is mundane. Everything and everyone has a purpose.

As you read this final chapter, I hope you will recognize God or at least give yourself a chance to search out the truth about Him. Whether you believe in Him or not, you are a part of a bigger plan. Everyone is included. You may express your own agenda and share personal stories, totally unaware that you are taking part in this grand scheme.

I hope when I reveal Rudy's biggest coincident, you will clearly see the truth and how God used Rudy through the time frame of eight years to change my life. Through this relationship with Rudy, I strengthened my faith in God and myself.

The truth of this story is not about winning a national championship. That was only the incentive to begin my adventure with

Rudy. Through this experience, I discovered I could set and achieve goals. I developed the confidence to overcome fears and insecurities. But most of all, I experienced love, agape love.

The truth is simple. There is more to the world than our limited knowledge can grasp.

I give considerable credit to Rudy. Through his quiet but bold personality, he inspired me to go the extra mile. He encouraged me to believe in myself and in him.

He enlightened me to evaluate my communication skills. I came to the realization that it is not always about speaking. It is about body language, noticing cues given off by animals and individuals. Communication is about accepting people and animals where you find them in life and working on communicating with them from there, forgetting any past experiences.

Most important, I learned to listen and not just with my ears but my heart as well. Listening is probably the biggest asset a person possesses, and learning to listen is a continual process that never ceases.

It would be several years before I put it all together and understood what had transpired in those eight years of training Rudy. It wasn't until the trip home that I began to understand the true purpose of this Tulsa trip.

We packed up and set out on the road, filled with the anticipation of being home. I think everyone felt the dread of the long ride home and mental fatigue from the whole experience. Whereas the adventure coming out was new and exciting, the trip home was filled with longing and exhaustion. For the most part, it was just miles of highways, gas stations, and rest stops.

We consumed a ton of fast food, drank gallons of coffee, and downed energy drinks. We all agreed to drive straight through this time, with no sleepover stop. The drivers would rotate between Colten and myself. The others would rotate sleep and wakefulness, observing the drivers for signs of fatigue.

I still hoped to see the Mississippi River, and that was enough of an incentive to keep me awake. Little did I know that we would arrive, just like the first trip, at midnight. It would be a future trip in 2015 before I finally saw the Mississippi River in the daylight.

Arriving at the Mississippi River Bridge at midnight found me desperate to use the restroom. Too much coffee and an old bladder pushed beyond its capabilities, found me waking Colten up from a much-needed nap. I needed help finding a restroom and quickly! Colten spotted a sign advertising the Memphis Welcome Center up ahead just after the bridge. Surely, they would have a restroom.

Following the signs to the Welcome Center, we ended up next to the Mississippi bridge base, close to the river. My urgency for relief had me stopping the truck, jumping out in the parking lot, and racing to the center's restrooms.

The abrupt stop woke everyone up, and they soon were discussing and planning the next possible break for gas or coffee while they waited on me. After all, we had 197 miles 'til we reached Nashville. Hopefully Colten would remember the few available stops.

Colten took over the driver's seat and turned the truck around.

As I grabbed the entrance doors, I just imagined the relief of a clean restroom. Unbelievable what happened next. The doors were locked!

"Lights were on, but nobody home," came to my mind. Holding til the next possible stop was not an option!

Desperately looking around, I spotted the bushes beside the entrance doors. Ducking down behind them, I immediately pulled my pants down and relieved my bloated bladder. Relief never felt so good. Now I could continue the journey without that annoying distraction.

As I approached the truck, everyone was laughing hysterically. I just assumed it was the fact that the doors were locked and I used the bushes as a bathroom. To my horror, they pointed to the Welcome Center Doors where there was a video camera recording the whole incident. I guess someone was going to get an eyeful and a good laugh the next day. Dalton and Colten said I would go viral on YouTube. Not the kind of notoriety I wanted. Wait 'til Dart hears about this one.

Back on the road, it was more of the same old thing over and over. After a boring 197 miles, we reached Nashville hours after midnight. We had the luxury of no traffic and made good time until

Colten tried to take a shortcut. We ended up in a beautiful old neighborhood on a dead-end road where we could see the highway below us.

I got out and cried. How were we going turn this large trailer around on a narrow two-lane street with cars parked everywhere? Colten told me to calm down, and he would handle it.

Colten seesawed back and forth between parked cars with everyone spaced out on the road to watch the truck, trailer, and parked cars. It took a bit of magical maneuvering and a lot of time, but we eventually had the trailer turn in the right direction. All I could think was how the poor, tired ponies must feel, having to endure this torturous back and forth motion.

Rudy, aka Sugar Boy

Now what? I don't remember this being part of the journey. Sugar and I are pretty exhausted. The excitement of the "new adventure" has worn off! We just want to go home. Unfortunately, I am sure we still have a ways to go.

I am relieved we don't have all the Nashville traffic like on the trip coming out to Tulsa. Must be the late hours keeping most of the people at home.

Let me see… It took us a full day and a half and a night to get out to Tulsa, so we should be arriving back home around ten or eleven in the morning, pending there are no more "Colten detours."

Was kind of funny seeing Mel using the bushes as a restroom at the Welcome Center stop. Bet she did not know I saw that! I admire the fact that she can be resourceful when needed.

Finally! I see they all are getting back in the truck. Looked like some kind of block party for a while. I appreciate Colten's driving abilities. Mel would have hit at least one car before she succeeded in turning around. I am sure glad everyone in the neighborhood stayed asleep and did not call the police. Wouldn't that been a big problem to explain.

Now, if he can just get us back to the highway and on the road again! "On the road again, just can't wait to get on the road again..."

Mel

Finally, we were on our way again. No more shortcuts!

When we arrived at the tunnels through the Blue Ridge Mountains, I felt like we were almost home. It was early dawn, and we were pleasantly surprised to see a black bear standing close to the entrance, enjoying his breakfast. That reminded me that we needed to do the same.

Arriving in North Carolina, we started looking for a place to exchange drivers and appease our appetites, preferably a restaurant with a big parking lot or a traveler's stop with gas and food. We all needed to stretch our legs, ponies included.

Eventually, we found a traveler's rest stop with gas and food. Everyone ate a quick breakfast, and I took over the driving. I was revived after the good food and overjoyed knowing we only had about two hours left to reach home.

Finally, we arrived home, safe and sound. Though we were weary from the trip, we still had to unload the truck and trailer. The work of a horse show is endless. I knew I had large amounts of clothes to wash and tack to separate and store away. But first, we needed to unload the exhausted ponies. I watched with joy as they bounded off, Rudy into his paddock and Sugar into the mare pasture. The first thing they did was roll as if to rub off all the exhaustion from the trip.

Back at the trailer, everyone pitched in and worked mindlessly like machines, only wanting to get the job completed. Before everyone left, I thanked them for the overwhelming assistance. I could not have accomplished it without them. I was especially appreciative of Dart, who had to work his job at the fire department and tend to the farm while we were away. A supportive husband, family, and friends came through for me. For this, I am forever grateful.

Now how do I process all the wonderful things I had experienced? I could not wait to share all the events I had experienced with my friends and family. Maybe a relaxing night at home would give me some insight into what just happened in my life. Mission accomplished. We had our national championship and a reserve championship. Now what?

After a good night's rest, our lives slowly returned to normal. The routine of work and farm duties restarted the cycle of normalcy. In fact, my life was a bit anticlimactic. I had achieved my dream.

In late October I received a call from my good friend, Janice Early, the Welsh pony breeder who owned Bailef. I had never received a call from her, so I was intrigued that she felt the need to talk with me.

"Hey, Mel. Hope everything is going good with you. I was really proud of you and Rudy. You had a really good show in Tulsa."

"Thanks, Janice. I was so impressed with the show. I still can't believe how well Rudy did. It was a dream come true for me. In fact, I hope we can support the show in the future as well, depending on our finances," I replied laughingly.

"Well, the main reason I called is… I thought you might be interested in what I just learned. Bailef's dam is on Craigslist for free! Thought you might seriously consider acquiring her for your breeding program. She is in her twenties, but you may be able to get at least one foal out of her," she explained.

"Are you kidding me?" I replied. "I would love to have her. But Janice, I can't come to Texas after going to Tulsa. I have no money!"

Janice said, "Let me look further into this. I may know some people heading your way, and they could bring her to a meeting place halfway. Could you meet halfway?"

Quickly I responded, "I may be able to do that. Thank you so much for thinking of me! I really think that would be a great cross! Let me know as soon as you can. Thank you, thank you, thank you! Talk with you later. Bye!"

Dart was going to kill me. Another pony in a pasture already overgrazed. I decided to approach him anyway once I found out the arrangements.

I received another call from Janice later that afternoon. This, too, was an exciting discovery.

"Hi, Mel. You don't have to worry about coming to Texas or even halfway. The mare is in Whiteville, North Carolina," Janice explained. "Do you know where that is?"

"Sure do. I can do that!" I replied. "We go to Holden beach for vacation, and we pass right through Whiteville on the way. It is about three or four hours from our house. Sure beats going to Texas." I laughed.

"Well, the owner had already given the mare away, but I am working on changing her mind. I feel you would give her a better home and opportunity," Janice explained. "I, too, would like to see that Rudy/Bailef cross. I really like Rudy, and I think we both have similar ideas about what is important in our breeding programs… athleticism and work ethic."

"I can do Whiteville!" I exclaimed. "I can do Whiteville! Hey, thank you for your confidence in Rudy and my breeding program. I am grateful for your support of him. Please…let me know as soon as you find out something. Talk to you later. Bye."

Once again, I was in limbo. I really wanted to see a Rudy/Bailef cross—two of my favorite stallions in the ancestry of a foal, and a half sibling to Bailef!

I soon acquired the knowledge that the family that wanted Rambur had small children. Rambur had been a brood mare her entire life and was not really suitable for small children. Janice was concerned about this possible situation. I was too.

It seemed like eternity before the phone rang. I prayed that Janice was successful in obtaining a deal. I worried about what Janice would say as I picked up the receiver.

"Hi, Mel," Janice sounded cheerful. Maybe that was a good sign. "Rambur is yours. You just need to come and get her as soon as possible. The owner really needs to move her. By the way, if you succeed in getting her bred, let me know. I would really like to see the foal. Talk with you later or email me. Bye."

As I hung up the phone, I could hear the relief in Janice's voice. Like me, she truly cares for her ponies.

After hanging up, I quickly approached Dart about the acquisition. He knew a little about Bailef but was not sure about bringing in an old mare. We really did not need another brood mare, especially one that might not produce and become just another mouth to feed.

Even so, Dart saw the belief and determination in my eyes and gave me the go-ahead to make arrangements to pick her up. This was a total turn of events for me. Never in my wildest dream would I have entertained the thought of owning Bailef's dam.

Dalton agreed to accompany me on the trip to Whiteville. She was becoming my constant companion in my many wild schemes to promote the farm. I appreciated the "ride-along buddy." I also trusted her with helping me load an unfamiliar mare.

On the way down, we discussed the possibilities of this new mare joining our brood mare band, which currently consisted of two grey mares and a red roan mare. They were well bred but had only achieved minor show records, and the greys were labeled as problem ponies for children.

Our mares were not mean but very naughty. Consistently they outsmarted young riders and frustrated the parents with their disobedient attitudes. Dalton and I both knew we could probably fix that problem and actually liked the fact that they were so clever.

We laughed about what this new mare's probability was on the "naughty" scale. We had not even seen a picture of Rambur, so this was going to be our first introduction to her. I figured if Janice had owned her, she must be okay.

We left early in the morning after feeding the ponies on a day that started out sunny. As we traveled east, we saw threatening clouds showing the possibility of a storm.

It was November 17, and we planned on arriving around 1:00 p.m. Christine Garrett, the owner of the farm, arranged to meet us. On her instructions, we drove through her gate and proceeded to the wooded area she had described, looking for her driveway and house.

Once we spotted her home, hidden in the woods, we parked the trailer and left the warmth of the truck and experienced the damp coolness of a November day. The temperature had really changed since beginning our trip.

Leaving the parked trailer, we were greeted by Christine. She explained that she was a realtor and how the real estate market had gone sour. Financially she had to reduce her herd. Rambur was a senior mare and required more upkeep, so she was the first choice to offer up for sale or give away. She also explained that Rambur's Reflection, Bailef's dam, was in poor condition as she just weaned a foal off her. Her condition might be due to her age or having the foal on her.

I understood and talked with her about how a foal on an older mare can really pull the mare's condition down. I was relieved to hear that she had been in foal recently. That should give me better odds of achieving a pregnancy with her in the spring.

Christine took us on a quick tour of her farm. I observed that most of her ponies were lovely and in good shape. There were ponies of all ages and sizes, and she educated us on their pedigrees and relationships.

She also informed us that most were not broke to ride, and she was in need of a possible trainer. My pony trainer "radar" quickly picked up on this fact. I had acquired all my broodmares through training services or trades of Rudy's foals. Always short on cash, I only had my services or foals to offer in a trade.

Having a good reputation as a trainer, I hoped I could convince Christine to consider a possible trade for a Rambur daughter that I had spotted amongst the youngster. Since we were already here, we could pick up the extra mare as well. This was provisional as we needed to work out a deal.

Pointing out a couple of young mares that I really liked, I offered her my services for training in a possible trade. Christine hesitated but replied that she really needed money and not services at this time. I quickly realized she did not know me, and even I would have been hesitant to deal with a stranger, regardless of my financial situation.

Eventually, she showed Rambur to us. She was a small grey mare who was underweight. She had good conformation, despite the lack of weight, and a pretty head with a large dark eye. I was not disappointed. She was worth the trip down. I hoped we could put some weight back on her before the spring.

After loading her on the trailer, Christine invited us into her home to sign the registration papers over to us. As she went through her files, I thought I should explain what I had planned for Rambur. Feeling a bit proud of what Rudy had accomplished at the nationals, I decide to brag a little. As she pulled out Rambur's papers, I told her that I wanted to breed my "national champion" stallion, Blueridge Rising Star, to her next spring. I also explained that I was a big Bailef fan and was so excited to be able to have his mom join our broodmare band.

Before I could continue my story about Rudy winning his championship, Christine replied, "Oh, I know Rudy."

Hot dog! We were finally making strides in the Welsh Breed. Here was a complete stranger who actually knew him. It must be his national championship win. Tulsa was the right move to make, and now it was paying off.

She then added, "I was the first one to own him. In fact, I named him Blueridge Rising Star. I decided to called him Rudy, his barn name."

I was dumbfounded.

"I originally bought him in utero on his pedigree," she explained. "When he was three weeks old, I had an accident and broke both my arms training a pony. I was looking at weeks in casts and physical therapy, and I knew I had to give him back." She continued, "No way could I have handled a weanling."

I could not believe what I was hearing. I was so astonished; my mouth fell open, and nothing came out. I reflected back on all the coincidences and situations that had to transpire in the eight years between the first time I saw Rudy at three weeks old and the Welsh Pony and Cob Society American National Show in 2014.

First there was the arrival of the Select Pony Sale brochure to introduce me to the Welsh pony breed. After the disillusion I had felt from my previous breed association, the timing on this one had to be perfect.

Next was the discovery of Blueridge Welsh Pony Farm and the introduction to Harmony Dowman, where I first saw Rudy at three weeks old. I remembered the disappointment I experienced after learning he was already sold.

Between the time I first encountered Rudy and the three-week time period before I took our mares up for breeding, Christina had to have her unfortunate accident that allowed me to propose a deal to acquire Rudy.

Thirdly was the encounter with Janice Early, both in Raleigh at the AGM and again through writing the magazine article, "Welsh, Not Just for Kids." This article featured Bailef as one of my examples of adults riding ponies successfully in sporting events.

At the AGM convention, we also officially met John Almond, the judge who encouraged me by purchasing Rudy's stud fee donation. He also educated and mentored me when I was so new to the Welsh breed. John would also later put out the email with the info on Rambur's Reflection, who was advertised on Craigslist.

Finally, the timing on the death of my mother and the settlement of her estate in August of 2014. This allowed the financial support to attend the American National Welsh show.

Through eight years of dreaming, scheming, and pursuing what I perceived as my dream, God actually led me to the biggest "coincidence" ever, the one that would forever change my outlook on life.

Everything became crystal clear. Step by step, God introduced me to people and situations that not only helped me grow in my faith and my confidence but showed me a real purpose in life. They say hindsight is twenty-twenty, and I wholeheartedly agree.

I now see the plan God had in mind for Rudy and me. Looking back, I recognize the "coincidences" that gave me reason to pause and actually open my eyes to another perspective. He utilized Rudy to inspire me to write, to follow my dreams, and to seek more out of life.

By using this wonderful pony, I was inspired to encourage people to continue dreaming and to pursue and believe in the impossible. I now wanted to assist people in overcoming their fears. I wanted to encourage others to move out of the mere existence of what the world dictated as normal.

I have often been called "intuitive," and I now embrace this aspect of my personality. It helps me believe in the imperceptibility as well as the actuality.

In fact, my views and life will never be the same. I thank God, and I thank a very special Welsh pony named Rudy for showing me the way and sustaining me while pursuing my dream. I believe that God uses whatever it takes to get you where you need to be…even if it is a mischievous Welsh pony.

I have said many times in the past and will continue to say in the future, "I don't believe in coincidences."

Albert Einstein just says it best: "Coincidences are just God's way of staying anonymous."

About the Author

Melanie Bell has been a successful certified open horse show judge for over twenty-seven years. She is a Welsh judge and has attended the American National Welsh Pony and Cob show four times, winning several national and reserve national championships.

Melanie participated in riding clinics with renown horse trainers, John Lyons and Ray Hunt. She credits these successful horsemen for enlightening her to the horse's perspective.

Melanie is an award-winning artist who specializes in watercolor, sculpture, and graphite pencil renderings. Her clients include the Charlotte International Airport, Tom Fowler, and numerous horse farms.

Her equine articles have been published by *The Welsh Journal*, *The Carolina Hoofbeats*, and *The Pony Quarterly*.

Sugar Boy, aka Blueridge Rising Star, has been chosen twice to represent the Welsh pony breed in 2020 *Horse Illustrated* magazine editions. He also represented the Welsh pony breed in the 2014 North Carolina State Fair's Year of the Horse program.

Melanie and her husband, Dart, reside at Dartland Farms in Iron Station, North Carolina, where they currently raise their champion Welsh ponies.

CPSIA information can be obtained
at www.ICGtesting.com
Printed in the USA
BVHW032246291022
650534BV00006B/113